Sacred refuge

Why and How to Make a Retreat

Sacred refuge

Why and How to Make a Retreat

THOMAS M. SANTA

ave maria press AᴍP Notre Dame, Indiana

---

www.avemariapress.com

International Standard Book Number: 1-59471-052-X

Cover and text design by John Carson

Cover photo © Brand X Pictures /Punchstock

Printed and bound in the United States of America.

Library of Congress Cataloging-in-Publication Data

Santa, Thomas M., 1952-
    Sacred refuge : why and how to make a retreat / Thomas M. Santa.
        p. cm.
    ISBN 1-59471-052-X (pbk.)
    1. Spiritual retreats--Catholic Church. I. Title.

    BX2375.A3S26 2005
    269'.6--dc22
                                        2004026534

To the people of the Spiritual Life Center in Wichita, Kansas, and to the people of the Redemptorist Renewal Center in Tucson, Arizona. Places of sacred refuge in which I have been privileged to serve, to learn, and to experience the powerful presence of God.

CONTENTS

PART **ONE**

WHY?

CHAPTER ONE

A CHOICE
AND A DECISION

When you lose touch with inner stillness, you lose touch with yourself. When you lose touch with yourself, you lose yourself in the world.
— Eckhart Tolle

I carried inside me a cut and bleeding soul, and how to get rid of it I did not know. I sought every pleasure—the countryside, sports, fooling around, the peace of a garden, friends and good company, sex, and reading. My soul floundered in the void— and came back upon me.
— Saint Augustine, *Confessions*

My soul spoke to me and said, "The lantern which you carry is not yours, and the song that you sing was not composed within your heart, for even if you bear the light, you are not the light, and even if you are a lute fastened with strings, you are not the lute player."
— Kahlil Gibran, *Thoughts and Meditations*

It is of the greatest importance to practice a regular period of withdrawal. When a person does not reflect on the real purpose of his life, what meaning is there to his existence?
— **Nahman of Bratslav**

The people who make it their business to track demographic trends and identify social movements inform us that there is in our technological and "first world" culture a growing interest in spirituality. There seems to be a developing sense and growing awareness that an essential component of the human experience is missing. The babyboomers, the generation that has dominated the social landscape for so long, have become restless again. This time the restlessness is not necessarily driven by the need to achieve or succeed, the need to invest or divest, but may rather be focused on a more personal need: the search for meaning and integration, some kind of answer to the ultimate question of life, "Why am I here? What is my purpose?"

In response to the collective groan, the questions, and the search, there is a predictable response to the perceived demand. Resort hotels construct spas where the body can be prodded, poked, stretched, and pulled. Health club personnel encourage their patrons to lift, press, spin, and then repeat the rotation. The diet gurus preach about the benefits of low fat, high protein, low carbohydrate, and somehow balanced diets. People no longer thoughtlessly supersize their fast food orders while others pretend they are completely filled, with no room left to conclude a meal with desert, no matter how tempting the offering might be. Each of these decisions may be part of the answer, and may be a partial response to the perceived need, but they are not ultimately satisfying.

For every person who seeks meaning out of a weekend at a spa hotel, for every person who attempts to fill an inner emptiness by increasing their aerobic activity or decreasing their caloric intake, for each of these there are others who discover another response. These people, well over 2.5 million people in North America each year, seek out not the new and the trendy, but rather the old and the traditional. Millions of people have ignored the consumer and market shrines of our popular culture and seek rather places of sacred refuge. In the process of discovery they are introduced to a life of integration and wholeness and begin to understand the relationship between the physical, the intellectual, and the spiritual components of the human person.

Traditional and not so traditional places of sacred refuge, places where the spiritual person can be nourished and where the body, the mind, and the spirit are understood as integrated and mutually important, dot the landscape. A collection of more than two thousand monasteries, abbeys, retreat centers, renewal centers, and hermitages have been registered and catalogued. Many are situated in out of the way places or perched on the edge of the frantic activity of large metropolitan areas. Most, if not all, welcome guests who arrive for a short period of time, a day or a weekend, as well as others who choose to extend their stay for as long as possible.

Each of the major religious traditions, more often than not the sponsors of the places of sacred refuge named above, have long encouraged the rituals, exercises, and specific components of their spiritual tradition. Most religious traditions have routinely set aside resources (money, buildings, and personnel) that can be used for the spiritual practices and exercises that are required by their members. In a very real sense these sacred places, quietly present but off the radar for many years, have now come into focus for a general population who for so long may have been unaware of their existence and purpose.

I am a privileged person because I am in permanent residence in one of these sacred refuges. I live and work at a retreat and renewal center in Tucson, Arizona, tucked below the Tucson Mountains with a sweeping view of the city stretching out below us. I live in a place of destination, a sacred place made holy by the "picture rocks," the Petroglyphs, that were long ago etched into the nearby rock formations by the Hohokam people. No one knows why the ancients came to this particular point in the Sonoran Desert, but there seems to be something about this place that nourishes life and brings people to a point of contact with something or someone that they understand to be spiritual.

Today, a thousand years after the Hohokam first arrived, it continues to be a sacred place where people from all over the world gather. Each person who arrives at our registration desk has made the necessary choices and decisions, set aside some of their precious time out of a busy week, and accumulated the funds that they need in order to meet the costs of a retreat experience. Not exactly the same procedure that the Hohokam might have engaged in, but there are some similarities.

The retreat experience itself, the primary reason the people gather, is a personal choice to withdraw to a place of seclusion and silence for the purpose of spiritual renewal, an experience that comes in many different and varied formats. Some people come to the retreat center for a day, a few precious hours of silence and inactivity, where they are given the permission and provided the support to simply be still and silent, away from the television and the phone. Others come for an entire weekend, arriving a little bit harried on Friday afternoon, just in time for the evening meal, and then reluctantly leaving on Sunday, after brunch, some extending their time for just a few minutes longer. Still others come for a week or more, sometimes in order to learn a new spiritual skill, other times to participate in some kind of activity for their own personal growth and development, and still other times simply to be quiet, uninterrupted, and focused on their relationship with God.

Every day from my office window I observe people quietly making their way to the chapel, which in our retreat center occupies the central and most prominent location. I see people outside walking slowly on one of the many paths that penetrate the desert landscape, taking a moment to stop and examine a cactus or perhaps to observe a lizard, or if they are really blessed, to watch a rattlesnake slowly wind his way through the desert in search of some cool place to rest. Still others make their way down to the Labyrinth and spend an hour or more slowly walking, meditating, and praying until they reach the center. I have observed people sit at the center of the Labyrinth and weep, I have observed others simply sit and smile.

On some days, before the sun becomes too hot, I watch the resident Zen students, dressed in black, taking their "walking meditation" between their formal and ritualized periods of sitting. They slowly follow each other, adopting a certain cadence and pace that is not only meditative for them but which also somehow seems to make everyone around them more quiet and reflective.

Day in and day out I am privileged to listen to people who choose to share with me their spiritual journey. They talk about their joys and their disappointments. They share with me insights that they have arrived at about important relationships in their lives. They talked about slowly arriving at a point in their life when they have come to a personal awareness that they are truly blessed. At other times they share with me the details of the struggle that comes with facing the silence that is necessary for prayer and meditation. How difficult it can be for them to sit quietly, to attempt to lay aside their thoughts and other distractions, and to concentrate on their breathing, the life breath of the spirit that moves through them.

A retreat center is a place of quiet and solitude. It is a place where the everyday rhythms of life are deliberately disrupted, a place where people choose to disengage their automatic pilot in order to assume manual control of their thoughts, feelings, and emotions, only slowly learning to let go of control, that core illusion of the human experience, placing all that they are and hope to be into the heart and mind of the Other whom they understand to be God.

The decision to seek out a retreat center, a place of sacred refuge, is a choice and a decision that is rooted in the experience of life. It is a decision that can be made for a variety of reasons, some of which may be defensive, still others which may be explorative or merely curious. Regardless of what may propel a person to seek to incorporate the experience of a retreat into their life, all who make such a decision ultimately are introduced to a process that is life nourishing and even life changing.

The process that is described here, however, is ongoing. It is not accomplished within the time period of a single retreat weekend, or, for that matter, even an extended retreat. The retreat experience introduces you to the process, offers specific skills and practices that will enable and encourage the process, and finally provides an atmosphere that is conducive to growth. The retreat experience does not, however, guarantee the end result. It is only through continued practice, discipline, and patience that the fullness and the riches of the spiritual practice are slowly revealed and experienced.

The reflection that follows is presented from a Christian perspective and is rooted in the Roman Catholic tradition. It is so because the only authentic way that I can speak about the process is from my own experience, and that experience is Catholic and Christian. However, that being noted, the elements are not exclusive to the Christian tradition but are rather much more universal. Other spiritual traditions may not use the same words to describe the experience but there will be recognition of the process and more than likely an assent of the end result.

CHAPTER **TWO**

THE CALL TO JOURNEY AND TO SEEK THE OTHER

Ask, and it will be given to you; seek and you will find; knock
and the door will be opened to you.
—Matthew 7:7

*God leads the child he has called in wonderful ways. God
takes the soul to a secret place, for God alone will play with it
in a game of which the body knows nothing. God says, "I am
your playmate! Your childhood was a companion
of my Holy Spirit."*
—Mechtild of Magdeburg

*To seek is as good as seeing. God wants us to search earnestly
and with perseverance, without sloth and worthless sorrow.
We must know that God will appear suddenly and joyfully to all
lovers of God.*
—Julian of Norwich

Thou takest the pen and the lines dance. Thou takest the flute—and the notes shimmer. Thou takest the brush—and the colors sing. So all things have meaning and beauty in that space beyond time where Thou art. How, then, can I hold back anything from Thee?
—Dag Hammarskjold

There is a possibility that one of the reasons that you desire to explore the great spiritual practice of retreats and are attracted to this book is that you may be experiencing something which is profound, important, and possibly even somewhat unsettling. Perhaps you have chosen to read these few pages in the hopes that you might experience an insight that will help you more clearly understand what you may be feeling. Know that you are not the first person to recognize such a change. In fact, you may be relieved to know that it is not at all uncommon and has been an integral part of the human experience for a very long time.

From the beginning of the human experience, human beings have always had within them a curiosity, a desire for what many spiritual masters might identify as the Other. At certain times in the human journey, when our ancestors were preoccupied with survival, the curiosity might have not been acted on, while at other times it seems to have been a preoccupation, something that engaged their imagination, their feelings, and the deepest part of themselves. As a result of the human response and recognition of the Other we are able to look back from where we have come and recognize manifestations of this experience through form, presence, or elaborate ritual in the thousands of years of our existence.

It is impossible to pinpoint the first moment in the human journey when this awareness and desire for the manifestation of the Other was first acted upon. However, whenever it first happened, whenever the first human person became aware that there was something or someone greater than himself or herself, the human person started the process of seeking to know more, to understand more, and ultimately to seek some sort of union or relationship with the Other. Ultimately, of course, when the human person took the necessary time to begin this process of seeking, the realization soon dawned on the original seeker that the one whom he or she was seeking seemed to be returning the favor: the seeker was also being pursued.

Perhaps the ancestral person, important in the three great monotheistic religions of our day—Christianity, Judaism, and Islam—might best illustrate the dynamic. In the story of Abraham, told for us in the Hebrew scriptures in the book of Genesis and repeatedly referenced in the Koran, we are introduced to a Bedouin nomad who seeks to respond to the stirrings within him. We do not know for certain that Abraham's quest was primarily a spiritual quest but we do know that his story has all of the components that are traditionally considered necessary in order to engage in such a journey.

According to the story, Abraham seems highly motivated to find and establish a relationship with the Other. The Koran tells us that from his earliest childhood experiences he sensed the presence of the Other, whom he identified as the "one God" and he desired to serve only this presence he assumed to be divine. In a world filled with many gods, with many spiritual paths, Abraham remained clearly focused on his pursuit and succeeded in establishing a communication with the God whom he pursued. In the Torah, where we meet Abraham not as a child but as an old man, we are brought into the story at seemingly the most dramatic junction, the point where obvious communication had been established and a certain familiarity was also present. This dramatic moment is known as the covenant between Yahweh and Abraham, effectively ratifying the relationship for all time: "I will be your God and you will be my people" (Gn 17:4–8).

What is missing from all of the stories that we have about Abraham is the process that he personally engaged in during this pursuit. We are not told of the countless hours of reflection. We are not told of the wonderings, the doubts, and the questions that would necessarily be part and parcel of an experience moving from an acceptance of the many gods of polytheism to the one God of monotheism. It would not have been easy to lay aside old habits and beliefs, and to convince others to do the same, without a conviction formed deep within, a conviction that would eventually manifest itself into a belief, a strongly held value that would animate the rest of his life and define his relationships.

It is this process, today what we might identify as the movement of the spirit of a person from one point of view to another, which is central to our understanding of the seeker seeking, the journey to the Other, or within the context of this book, the experience of a retreat. Although the process is not necessarily limited to the spiritual journey, after all the movement of the spirit from one point of view to another is possible in many different areas of life, it is essential for the spiritual journey. Perhaps, it is for this reason that the concept of a retreat usually suggests and emphasizes the spiritual quest above all.

Today, for most people, the spiritual quest does not begin on a windswept plain, surrounded by herds and family, as it did for Abraham, but the quest is just as significant and essential. It may be asserted that it might be more difficult for the modern person to consider such a journey. More often than not, in a world filled with myriad distractions, voices, images, and potential choices, the single most difficult decision might be to identify the stirrings—or as some traditions name it, the "call" within us—as something that is spiritual. We might even name it something else, in all sincerity and in our belief that we have correctly identified what is going on within oursleves. As a result, instead of recognizing the stirring within as a spiritual moment and embarking on a spiritual quest, we might turn to a different job, or believe that our primary relationships are stale and no longer life giving and therefore seek to change our commitments. Still others of us will turn to therapy, a new exercise program, the latest diet, or something new and trendy, never considering the possibility that what is going on within us might well be the ancient call of the Other who seeks us.

Alphonsus Liguori, a saint and spiritual teacher who lived in the eighteenth century, referenced in his many spiritual writings that "we desire because first we have been desired." In other words Alphonsus believed, as do many other spiritual teachers, that there is within us an innate call, an invitation, or perhaps just a stirring, that orientates the human person toward spiritual wholeness and unity. We respond to this innate part of ourselves at different times in our life and for many different reasons. Perhaps one of the reasons you chose this particular book is because you are open to taking the necessary steps to respond to the desire that you feel within yourself.

If you sense that you have arrived at a point in life where you feel a need within yourself that cries out to be attended to, you may well be moving to a point of change or movement, responding to what we have identified as the call of the Other. If you are tired of all of the old ways of thinking, if the distractions that once succeeded in "getting you through the day," no longer seem to be working, you may well be responding to an ancient stirring within that is calling you to become aware of life in a completely different way. If you find yourself listening to another person and nodding in agreement, all the while believing that there is something more, the "yes, but" of life, you may well be experiencing an invitation and a call to a deepening spiritual growth and development. If this restlessness is from the Holy One, if it is truly a spiritual call and invitation, it will not simply disappear or go away, some sort of response will be required of you.

21

It is this feeling, the sense as a human person that there is something more to life, which propelled Abraham many centuries ago. It is the foundational experience of the spiritual journey, the first step, and if responded to, a step that will lead you on a path to the Holy One, God, the Sacred, or however you understand the Other. It is a wonderful journey, a journey that will lead to the fullness of health, wholeness, and holiness. It is also a journey that many other people, in all different faith traditions, are in the process of embarking on. Some have been on the journey for a long period of time while others have just made their first small steps. Regardless, it is important to know and understand, that no one has completed the journey. It is ongoing and there is not a time when a person can proclaim that they have arrived, that the journey is finished, and there is nothing more to discover or to appreciate. The spiritual journey is an eternal quest.

For many people, once the stirring within them is recognized and they determine that they will respond, attendance at a sponsored program at a retreat center is one of the first steps taken. It can be a little overwhelming at first, navigating your way through the various offerings and formats that are pretty standard at most centers, but it should not be discouraging. More often than not the personnel of a retreat center, who are also people on the spiritual journey, will be more than happy to help you select something that will be useful for you as you begin. Retreat personnel, not unlike the helpful and informed sales person at a favorite local bookstore, are often staff members because of their personal love for the product, in this instance spirituality. Their dedication, their interest, and their continuing commitment to spiritual growth will all contribute in positive ways to your own search for direction. You can approach a member of the retreat staff with the confidence of knowing that you will be accepted, encouraged, and hopefully pointed in the right direction.

CHAPTER THREE

AWARENESS: LEARNING TO FOCUS YOUR ATTENTION

When we sit, we know we are sitting. When we walk, we know we are walking. When we eat, we know we are eating.
—Buddha

When one's thoughts are neither frivolous nor flippant; when one's thoughts are neither stiff-necked nor stupid, but rather are harmonious, they habitually render physical calm and deep insight.
—Saint Hildegard of Bingen

Thomas Merton, a Trappist monk and mystic, a person whose writings are often referenced by people of many different faiths and traditions, once made the point that one of the most critical spiritual challenges of our day, of our time and place, is that we are too efficient, too focused on work, and too pragmatic, spending all of our time keeping the factory and the business running, leaving little time and energy for anything else. It is quite remarkable that he made this observation over thirty-five years ago, but the truth of the statement rings ever truer to us today.

For many people there are simply too many demands on their time, demands that they are required to perform in order to make ends meet. The time is necessarily dedicated to work, but also for a growing number of people there is the daily commute that brings them to their workplace, along with the commitments of raising a family and sustaining a relationship, maintaining the household, and the other routine tasks that consume the day, often bringing them to a point of exhaustion at the end of the day. Once they arrive home at the end of the workday, their bodies are tired, their minds are to the point of where it is impossible to concentrate and reflect, and their spirit is often drained. In this state of mind and spirit, all they want to experience is some kind of relief, literally to find something that will relax them, distract them, fill in the few hours before it is time for bed and they start the entire routine all over again.

As if the grind of the daily routine is not challenging enough, there is often a fear that also seems to be part of the experience, a fear indirectly referenced by Thomas Merton. The fear is the feeling of anxiety and unrest that is the result of slowing down, taking a breath, and changing the scenery for any length of time. This fear is present not because the human person does not yearn for such an experience and would not enjoy it, but rather because of the belief, and not without some basis for it, that if they choose to take time for themselves there is the very real possibility that their career might be affected, they might miss the crucial meeting, or perhaps be perceived as not dedicated enough or not truly orientated to success. For this reason even time away from the office or the workplace demands that a person check their voice mail and e-mail, in order to keep in touch with the latest developments or the next opportunity.

Unfortunately, this experience of life, sometimes jokingly referred to as the "rat race," is all too common and is the ordinary experience of life for many people. With this scenario in play, and often even assumed as the norm, it should also come as no surprise to anyone that this perception of what is normal and routine, what is expected and assumed, would also manifest itself in other experiences of life and not just in the workplace.

For example, many of our churches, the place where religious expression and worship is assumed to take place, have become mirror images of the culture. Instead of traditional places of silence, prayer, and reflection, some communities have become another kind of distraction, complete with rock, pop, or hip-hop choirs performing back-up to a biblical pop-psychologist preacher who is there more for the entertainment rather than instruction of a congregation lounging in plush sofas. Of course this routine cannot last forever: the presentation needs to be slick in order to get the congregation "in and out" within an agreed upon time limit, generally about an hour. In this context, it is quite possible to attend a church service and never experience one prolonged moment of silence or inactivity. The church, instead of being an oasis from the stress of living, the place where a clear identification of those things that are most important to us should be reverenced and cultivated, instead contributes to the overall feeling of being disconnected and out of touch. There is an immediate satisfaction to the participant, at the very least the satisfaction of knowing that they have responded to the spiritual and religious part of their personhood, but the feeling and the satisfaction often wears off and is not sustainable.

More and more people, as a result of their daily lives and the real scarcity of the experience of stillness, have learned to mistrust silence, inactivity, and solitude, in effect they have learned to mistrust those times in their life when there is seemingly nothing going on. Without some kind of background noise or some sort of image flashing before their eyes they become quickly uncomfortable. The mistrust of inactivity, for example, can easily be demonstrated through the observance of two very common occurrences.

25

Observe the behavior of people in their cars as they wait for a traffic light to change—especially if the light is a little longer than they expected—and notice how impatient and angry many people get: Road rage is one extreme example of this syndrome. Or observe people as they stand in line in the grocery store or at the movie theatre, especially if the line is not moving fast enough. Notice how quickly they attempt to fill the time by picking a magazine off the rack, by rearranging the food in their grocery cart, or by calling someone on their cell phone. Many people find it almost impossible to just stand quietly and patiently wait their turn.

Spiritual masters of most disciplines and all kinds of faith traditions insist that an important and a crucial step in the spiritual journey is to become aware of life and to learn how not to avoid inactivity but to actually seek it out. The masters gently, and sometimes not so gently, prod their students to become aware of the choices and the decisions that they make each day, to become aware of all that simply passes them by at any given moment because of the inability to focus their attention and to become comfortable with the time that it takes to truly be concentrated and in touch. Often, to concretely demonstrate this point and to teach the necessity of it, spiritual masters will assign their students a seemingly simple task to illustrate the difficulty of focusing their attention and becoming fully aware of what is happening around them. One such example is to try to fully enjoy every aspect, every nuanced taste and delightful smell, of food or beverage of their choice.

In order to participate in this simple learning activity, pick out something that you like to eat or drink, sit down with the chosen beverage or food, and try and focus your attention on what you are consuming. Spend a couple of minutes simply enjoying what you are doing, all the while resisting the temptation to figure out what the task is supposed to teach you. Only after you have spent these precious moments enjoying your food or drink begin the process of reflecting on what just occurred. Identify your feelings about what you just did. Was the attempt to focus your attention something that you found difficult to accomplish or did it come quite easily to you? Were you surprised at the speed or the slowness of the passage of time during this activity? Each of the answers that you provide to these simple questions will give you a beginning insight into what the spiritual masters define as "awareness."

In order to appreciate the spiritual lesson that can be learned from this simple exercise, further reflection, provided from a non-Judaeo-Christian perspective, can be useful. For example, Thich Nhat Hanh, referencing the Buddhist tradition, relates in *Living Buddha, Living Christ* (Riverhead Books, 1995) that instead of awareness, or the concept of focusing your attention, something like mindfulness may be more helpful. Instead of the exercise being performed in isolation, it is performed again and again at every mealtime with the recitation of what is called the Five Contemplations. "This food is the gift of the whole universe, the earth, the sky, and much hard work. May we live in a way that is worthy of the food. May we transform our unskillful states of mind, especially that of greed. May we eat only foods that nourish us and prevent illness. May we accept this food for the realization of the way of understanding and love." The praying of the Five Contemplations, the focused attention, deliberately eating at a slowed pace, and the awareness and mindfulness of what you are doing, all can contribute to your understanding and appreciation of a valuable spiritual lesson.

This kind of spiritual exercise is intended to bring a person face to face with a spiritual truth. Many people, or so it has been often observed, spend much of their day worried about the past or anticipating the future, very few live in the present moment, fully aware of what they are doing at any given moment. As a result of not living in the present moment, of not being open to the "now," a tremendous amount of energy must be devoted to maintaining a distracted, unfocused lifestyle. Unfortunately human beings, especially in our "first world" societies, have become accustomed to the expenditure of this kind of energy and assume that it is normal. Even more unfortunately it would seem that the prevailing culture encourages and supports a lifestyle of distraction and resists most attempts to focus the individual person's attention on any specific event or experience. In a very real sense, people have become consumers of the events, the experiences, and the choices and decisions of their lives, but this consumption is performed with little or no awareness of what may actually be happening.

A necessary step on the spiritual journey is for the human person to learn to resist the driving force of the culture in which we live and to become aware of the fact that life can be substantially different than how it is experienced at this moment. A major component of this step is to recognize that the individual person has a choice; the choice to come to an awareness, a deliberate and focused awareness where all your attention is heightened on the everyday events and experiences of your life, from the most profound to the supposedly inconsequential.

A not uncommon first response when a person first hears this suggestion is to assume that it is some sort of "crazy talk" and therefore to ignore it or brush it off, as the Greeks told the apostle Paul with some amusement, "We should like to hear you on this some other time" (Acts 17:32, *Revised Standard Version*). The temptation might be to dismiss the notion out of hand or try to categorize it as something that only a very few people are capable of achieving. Others might refer the suggestion to the arena of popularized hype while still others might label it as new age, anti-Christian, or "so much hocus pocus." Although this might be a person's first reaction, realize that when the spiritual masters are talking about becoming aware and learning how to focus our attention, they are not talking about "navel gazing," they are not talking about becoming totally self-centered and absorbed, and they are not talking about any particular change in your personal behavior that will be immediately noticeable, except, of course, to you.

Awareness, mindfulness, and focused attention are all about becoming a disciplined person: the choice to not let life just happen to you but rather to fully participate in the life that you are living. Awareness means coming to a place of openness, a place of unlimited potential, in order to begin the process of learning to perceive the integral nature of all things, events, and experiences, not for its own sake, but rather as a first step in the lifelong journey of becoming a whole, healthy, and holy person. In many spiritual traditions this step is recognized as responding to the invitation of the Other; in the Christian tradition it is understood as becoming cooperative with the grace offered to the individual person by God.

It might be difficult to admit, especially when we recognize the truth of the statement, that the individual human person is capable of living an undisciplined life. Often, when we reflect on it, we would assert that people who live a truly undisciplined life are people who are incapable of holding down a job, people who are imprisoned, or people who have life threatening problems with addictive behaviors or substances. Most of us, if the truth may be told, find a certain assurance in life that we are "not like them." For this reason it is very difficult to acknowledge that we too are undisciplined; our problems might not be as noticeable or even as destructive, but the problems are nevertheless present, even if we are unaware that they are.

All of us are ready to acknowledge that there are certain behaviors and substances that can be introduced into the body or adopted as a way of behaving that are truly harmful. The culture in which we live has adopted a whole perspective, a way of recognizing and identifying unhealthy habits that we mutually agree should be avoided, such as drunkenness, drug addiction, smoking, and compulsive eating or shopping, to name just a few. Each of us is educated enough to at least recognize the potential harm and danger to our personal health and well being that each of these habits is capable of producing within us. At the same time, we recognize that a person who is engaged in a habit that is commonly accepted as unhealthy "needs to be made aware of their destructive behavior," adopt a recovery program that breaks the bonds of the habit, and be returned to the road of wellness. However, there are a whole other range of habits that are commonly acknowledged as acceptable, but which are in fact capable of achieving the same kind of destruction, if not of our physical lives then most certainly our spiritual lives. Each of these habits has the same ability to distract, numb, and dull our awareness, and this is where the real difficulty can be discovered.

Examples of behaviors and substances that can truly affect our spiritual lives would include all of the destructive behaviors named above, but used in moderation, such as drinking not to the point of drunkenness but certainly to the cusp of drunkenness. Other examples that might not come easily to mind would be hours upon hours of watching television, hours and hours of window shopping "just for something to do," or continually munching on junk food without even being aware of what we might be eating. Still other behaviors that affect our spiritual life and are capable of producing the same kind of lack of awareness can be discovered in the strongly held perceptions, opinions, and judgments that we might hold and seldom give a second thought to, never noticing how they might affect other people or even mold our own behavior.

Leading a disciplined life, leading a life of awareness that enables us to walk the path of the spiritual journey, does not mean that we need to abandon or root out of our lives any of the behaviors outlined above, although in some instances it might well come to that. But it does mean that we need to be aware of what we are choosing, what we are doing, what we are believing, and why.

Often the person who desires to make a retreat is a person who has come to an awareness in their personal life that something has to change. Many times the person who comes to a retreat experience is a person who has performed some kind of inventory of their life. Not infrequently this inventory was taken in response to a specific event or experience in their life, possible a tragic event such as a sudden loss of a loved one or the realization that they have an unhealthy addiction. Such events force people to focus their attention on who they are as a person. Still others come on retreat who have engaged in this personal inventory, not so much as a result of any one event or circumstance, but as a result of a culmination of many different things, all leading them to a conclusion that they need time away in order to "sort out their life." Still others are attracted to the retreat experience because of the published theme or topic of the retreat has resonated within them. Regardless of how people arrive at the point in which they begin to think about the possibility of a retreat, each of them has arrived at the point because of a growing awareness of the need for something different.

Most people, when they arrive at a retreat center, have no real clear idea of the connection between their personal habits, choices, opinions, and the other events and experiences of their lives and their spiritual life. Unfortunately, the human person is quite capable of categorizing their spiritual life as a kind of special entity, something that has its own time and place, but usually not viewed as integral to the growth and development of who they are and what they are capable of becoming. As a result of this unfortunate categorization, they do not realize that for a truly happy, whole, and healthy life there needs to be a strong integration between the physical, the psychological, and the spiritual. For many people, the experience of a retreat will be the first time in their lives that someone helps them make this connection.

The second step on the spiritual journey, after the initial call is recognized and acted upon, is to learn to develop the skills and become personally convinced of the necessity of focusing your attention, awareness, or mindfulness, which will lead to a more disciplined life. It is in the discipline, the daily awareness of the need to fully participate in life and not experience it as something that just happens to you, that leads a person to the next step of the journey.

CHAPTER **FOUR**

AWAKENING: THE MOVEMENT FROM LESS TO MORE

Spirituality means waking up. Most people, even though they don't know it, are asleep. . . . They never understand the loveliness and the beauty of this thing that we call human existence.
—Anthony de Mello, S.J.

If the inner self is awakened it communicates a new life to the intelligence where it lives, so that it becomes a living awareness of itself. And this awareness is not something that we have, but something that we are. It is a new and indefinable quality of our living being.
—Thomas Merton

A man approached the Buddha curious about his teachings and his life. The man asked the Buddha, "Who are you? Are you a man?" "No," the Buddha replied. "Are you God?" "No, I am not God." In frustration the man then challenged the Buddha, "Who are you then, neither man nor God?" "I am awake," the Buddha replied.
—Buddhist story

Once you have arrived at a point of decision in your life, that point which we have identified as awareness or mindfulness, you will soon recognize that there are certain choices and decisions that are necessary. Often the choices and the decisions that are now required are completely different from what you may have been accustomed to. For example, it might not be as easy at the end of the workday, no matter how tired you might be, to simply turn on the television and wait for the numbing effect of the images to take over. Simply put, this may no longer seem like a viable option, and you may even find yourself wondering how you could have literally wasted so much time when you did choose this as an option.

If part of your spiritual journey up to this point has already included some type of retreat experience, and the experience included the opportunity to spend some quality time with a retreat director, you may have been provided with certain spiritual exercises and resources that help you to continue to progress. At this point in the journey it is necessary to commit yourself to the regular practice of these spiritual exercises. For the person who has not yet enjoyed a retreat experience or committed to a spiritual exercise or regular practice an alternate decision might be to pick up a book on a spiritual topic, or perhaps a sacred text from your religious tradition. Another choice might simply be the decision to not read or do anything, but rather to sit and be comfortable with the sights and the sounds that are naturally present to you.

Today in the world in which we live, another option, which is not at all unusual, is to turn to the World Wide Web and put the power of a search engine to work. Words that might suggest themselves as necessary for the search could include awareness, mindfulness, focused attention, and eventually perhaps even retreat. Each of these words will produce a variety of results, introducing you to some of the language and the conceptual framework of the spiritual journey.

If the most attractive option in this turns out to be gathering information about a specific retreat format or a retreat center that seems inviting, you may find yourself drawn to a particular topic, workshop, or for that matter even a particular director or presenter. All the while however, while the research is something that engages your attention, there should also be a parallel experience of actually beginning to use the spiritual skill that has brought you to this step on the spiritual journey. A list of Web sites that may be helpful on your journey is listed on page 141.

A person who has entered into a process, who has taken the beginning steps on the journey to grow in awareness, may well spend an extended period of time not just searching for answers and directions, but also practicing the skill of actually focusing their attention. There is no correct timetable that is required, and the progress that a person makes is unique to his or her own situation and life experience. Eventually, however, a person begins to take the next step on the journey and begins a movement that will lead ever deeper into the spiritual experience. Part of this movement will be the process of recognition, followed by a commitment to learning about the spiritual journey as it has been played out in other people, at different times and places, and sometimes in references and resources very familiar to the reader.

For example, the Christian scriptures are filled with events, experiences, and teaching stories that are intended not only to inspire the reader to respond to the word of God, but also to provide us with insight and direction in our spiritual journey. The sacred books and scriptures of all spiritual tradition, each in their own way and from their own perspective, do the same. Spiritual masters, emerging from their own traditions, attempt to illustrate and bring to our attention key concepts that they have learned in their spiritual quest that will hopefully teach us about spirituality and the spiritual journey. Certain examples from the teaching of Jesus will perhaps be useful to illustrate this point.

In the gospel of John, challenged by the seemingly ever present and critical chorus of the Scribes and the Pharisees, Jesus attempts to answer a question that they put to him by stating, "Whoever follows me will never walk in darkness, but will have the light of life" (Jn 8:12). In another place, this time teaching his own disciples, Jesus states, "Your eye is the lamp of your body. If your eye is healthy, your whole body is full of light; but if it is not healthy, your body is full of darkness. Therefore consider whether the light in you is not darkness" (Lk 11:34–35). In each instance, and in many other examples that can be easily discovered in the Christian scriptures, Jesus pushes his audience to see life in a new way, to focus their attention and learn to appreciate the little things in life, to "look at the birds in the air," (Lk 12:24, *Revised Standard Version*), not only to appreciate the little things, but also to learn to step back from the details of life and understand how they are related to the bigger picture, for the birds "neither sow nor reap, they have neither storehouse nor barn, and yet God feeds them" (Lk 12:24). With such straightforward teachings and encouragement, Jesus challenged his audience to learn a simple lesson. In the dynamic proposed, people can understand the necessity of focusing their attention and then stepping back to see how all of life is related and integrated. As in the teachings of any great teacher, some people were able to respond and to understand and others were incapable.

The Christian scripture propose, but unfortunately the proposal can often become lost in the dogmatic translations and interpretations of the text, a challenging spiritual lesson. When people determine that they will try to live their lives in such a manner, that they will understand life as not just something that happens to them but rather as a gift that demands their active participation and awareness, they become people "not of the darkness but of the light."

The moment when this insight is awakened and claimed, when people begin to focus their attention and live a life of mindfulness, they experience the next step on the spiritual journey or, in the words of Jesus, they begin to experience the kingdom of God. It is also at this point that they are capable of beginning to understand one of the central teachings of Jesus, "For those who want to save their life will lose it, and those who lose their life for my sake, and for the sake of the gospel, will save it" (Mk 8:35).

The stories and teaching of Jesus are not the only reference point for this next step on the spiritual journey, identified in some traditions as the process of awakening and in still others as simply "waking up." Once you understand what you are looking for, the process can easily be identified in all kinds of people and in all kinds of circumstances. In each instance the process begins with focused attention and awareness but then goes a step further, recognizing how all of life is related and integrated, or to put it in another way, learning to recognize the "more instead of the less." A few other examples from the wide variety of human experience might be helpful.

In the science fiction classic *Dune* by Frank Herbert, there is a scene in which the hero-prince, by this time already a member of the Fremen community which is indigenous to the planet Dune, confronts the leader of the priestly class with the accusation, "You are unwilling to drink of the water of life because it brings you to a place where you dare not look." Of course the hero prince is willing to drink the water of life, he is willing to look into the place where the priestly class will not look, and as a result of his action, he experiences a profound change, "The sleeper has awakened." What the hero-prince experiences as a result of his awakening is the ability to integrate all of life and not just a small part of life; he is able to see the big picture and make the connections. When this integration and connection takes place he then experiences the movement of the "more instead of the less"; unfortunately the priestly class, a community that a person might assume would be masters of the spiritual journey, are incapable or perhaps unwilling to take the necessary steps on the spiritual journey and are trapped with the "less instead of the more."

In the Acts of the Apostles, a more familiar story of awakening is told, a story that is very familiar to a Christian audience. In this story, the Apostle Paul, on the road to Damascus, experiences some sort of encounter "with a voice from the heavens," a voice that Paul firmly identifies and believes to be the Risen Christ Jesus. We are not completely sure of all of the details, and there is obviously much more going on in this encounter than what is recorded in the Acts of the Apostles, but the end result is that Paul experiences a profound change in his life, and as the scripture relates, "he sight was restored" (Acts 9:18), or, to put it in another way, he moves from the darkness, where he cannot see, into the light where he now can see. Again, his experience, as it is played out in his life from that moment on, is the experience of the "more instead of the less." He transforms from a fire-breathing persecutor of the Christian community to the inspired evangelist, the preacher of the Christ and all things universal and cosmic that relate to the person of Jesus.

But perhaps the most important spiritual story of awakening is the story of Prince Siddharttha Gautama, known as the Buddha. Approximately twenty-five hundred years ago, the Prince, or Bodhisatta (Buddha-to-be), was living a life of tremendous wealth and refinement in northern India where his every possible need or desire was immediately attended to by a servant. Despite his tremendous wealth, there was nevertheless within him a stirring, the desire for something more, an understanding of what true happiness was, a happiness that was not dependent on his "intoxication with life" but rather something much more profound. The specific questions that led him to begin his quest were the inevitability of aging, illness, and death. This led the

Buddha to discover, through his focused attention and meditation, a new understanding and truth that he then shared with others who also sought to be released from that which bound them to unhappiness. In a very real sense, the Buddha moved to an experience of the "more instead of the less."

Each of these examples, and there are many more examples that can be referenced from mythological literature and other spiritual traditions, are examples of what it means to move from the second step on the spiritual journey, becoming aware, to the third step on the spiritual journey, which is to arrive at a point where you experience a new way of seeing life. Obviously, this new way of seeing will be understood in a different way by a Christian, by a Buddhist, by a Muslim, and by a Jewish person, all of whom can remain focused in their spiritual tradition and nevertheless experience this step in their personal spiritual journey. Regardless of how they may understand or interpret the experience, there seems to be a common element to the experience that is essential to the spiritual journey.

When you experience what it means to be awakened, when you experience the movement from the "less to the more," you will immediately notice a few characteristics of the experience that will begin to bring you into an even more profound awareness well beyond what you might have ever imagined or perhaps even hoped for. Another spiritual exercise might be helpful to help illustrate this point.

Find a comfortable place, a place where you know you will not be disturbed or easily distracted. Once you become comfortable, imagine a time in your life experience in which you felt good. Sit with this experience of life for a few moments and pay attention to the feeling that it produces within you. Secondly, choose a life experience that was not particularly positive or life giving for you. Sit with this experience of your life for a few moments and pay attention to the feelings that it produced within you.

Contrast the good experience and the bad experience and the feelings that are associated with both experiences. Now return to both experiences, the good and the bad, and attempt to look at both, not from the narrow vision of how you might have felt, but try and look at the wider picture of how each of these events are part of the fabric of your life. Attempt to integrate the experience and make the connections.

The purpose of the exercise is to help you become aware of how you, as an individual person, create your own environment by the things that you choose to focus your attention on. When a person learns not only to focus on the details of life (awareness) but also is willing to take the second step and step back from the details and focus their attention on the whole moment (awakening), they become less driven by anxiety and emotion and become more open to the possibilities of life, and by extension, the possibilities of health and holiness. It is this experience that is the movement to what we have been identifying as "the more instead of the less."

Perhaps another helpful illustration of what happens in this process can be illustrated by recalling a popular movie of a few years ago. In the animated movie *Antz*, featuring the voices of Woody Allen, Sharon Stone, Gene Hackman, Sylvester Stallone, Christopher Walken and Jennifer Lopez, we are introduced to a worker ant that is literally just one small ant among thousands. This particular ant is struggling to find his identity, win the heart of the princess that he worships from afar, and eventually is even called upon to save the colony from impending doom. We are witnesses as the story unfolds and are soon snatched up in the frenzied activity of the colony, the struggle for power and for love, and the anxiety produced by the adventure and the journey that our ant hero embarks on.

As entertaining as the movie is, it is only at the very end of the movie that we are introduced to the profound spiritual lesson that *Antz* so beautifully illustrates for us. The camera moves away from the frenzied activity of the colony and we soon see that it is just a small anthill in the middle of a field. The camera pulls back a little bit more and we observe that the anthill is in fact in the middle of Central Park in New York, and when the camera keeps pulling back, even more of the city is revealed, then the surrounding countryside, and then eventually the earth itself, freely floating in space, surrounded by the universe. All is put into perspective very gently as the camera pulls back. But at the same time it is an extremely powerful lesson and provides a necessary perspective.

As you attempt to incorporate the spiritual practice of awakening in your life, you will recognize that you are slowly becoming a person who continues to try and put all of life into the proper perspective. You are becoming a person who is trying to live a life that is fully awake and engaged. You are becoming a person who is trying to freely choose to see the "more" of life instead of the "less" of life. Another way of understanding this might be to identify it as the process of trying to "see the big picture," and not to get bogged down in all of the little things and distractions of life. As this process is engaged in, and you continue to commit yourself to the pace and the rhythm of moving from the "less to the more," certain experiences seem to be present, at least two of which need some explanation.

One such experience that seems to be not at all uncommon is that you might begin to become aware of within yourself an almost insatiable appetite for knowledge and for a variety of different perspectives of life. As more and more connections are made, and as the experience of learning to integrate the events, the choices, and the judgments of life into a wider perspective becomes more natural, there is a kind of "intoxication of life" that is experienced. This experience is a distraction on the spiritual path, a lesson that has been referenced in the spiritual journey of the Buddha but it is certainly not limited only to his experience—

it is very much a distraction and a potential danger for each person on the journey.

A person who has entered into the process of experiencing the beginning stages of becoming awake often desires to read and study more about the spiritual experience. For example, you might become very interested in the many different forms and manifestations of spirituality that may be discovered in the different spiritual traditions of humanity. You might become a regular attendee at the different retreats that are sponsored by a retreat center. You might be often observed in the spirituality section of the bookstore looking for a book on a topic that has just captured your imagination. In a very real sense, you may become a consumer of spiritual thought, practices, and experiences, never seemingly arriving at the point where you experience some kind of fullness or satisfaction.

As the "intoxication" continues, another component of the experience may become more and more pronounced; a certain arrogance can also become present. It is the arrogance, the impatience, and the frustration that you can feel about the other people in your life that you may perceive as not making the connections they should be making or being unable to see clearly what the issue at hand might really be. In other words, people whom you perceive and judge as people who are not also on the spiritual journey. Sometimes this frustration can lead to real conflict and in some extreme cases it can even lead to an unfortunate set of circumstances and decisions that may end long-standing relationships or friendships. It does not have to happen like this, especially if you are receiving the necessary spiritual direction that is an important part of the process, but it nevertheless sometimes occurs.

Hopefully, with the right kind of direction, with a companion mentor who can help you navigate this part of the spiritual journey, this experience of intoxication and arrogance should be short-lived, but again there is no perfect timetable. Ultimately, although it may be difficult to understand and imagine when it is first experienced, both of these experiences and steps on the journey are nothing more than footsteps on the path, they are most certainly not the place of completion or the place where the journey should end. Regardless of how a person might feel, and there is a wonderful and invigorating component in this step, that which is to come is even more powerful and even more life giving.

The spiritual masters tell a story that might be useful to illustrate this point. According to the story, an old monk is standing outside the monastery one day, when a younger monk asks him, "Why is it that so many people seemingly begin the spiritual journey but do not persevere in their quest?" At that moment a rabbit runs by in front of the master and the questioning monk pursued by a pack of dogs. There is a slight pause, and yet another pack of dogs comes running past them. The old monk smiles and looks to the younger monk and says, "Observe what happens next." Sure enough, after a few moments one of the dog packs returns to the village, yapping and barking all the while. The master tells the young monk, "That pack of dogs that just went by us again, yapping and barking, is the same pack of dogs that went by us a few minutes ago. This pack of dogs never saw the rabbit, they just heard the barking. And so it is with the spiritual journey. Some people start the journey but they never actually see the rabbit; as a result they soon grow tired and discouraged. In order to stay committed to the journey you actually have to see the rabbit, and not just follow the barking."

As you continue to walk the steps of the spiritual journey and progress in your practice, you should slowly sense within yourself a movement away from the experience of being intoxicated, the experience of arrogance, and the perceptions and the judgments that may result. This movement and progress can also be identified and understood as the movement from the "less to the more" and it is a powerful experience. If, on the other hand, there is no movement or progress and if you remain in the intoxicated and con-suming stage, you must become focused again—either you have taken your eyes off of the rabbit or in fact you never saw the rabbit and have just been following the barking.

CHAPTER FIVE

SEEKING SOLITUDE AND SILENCE

Whenever there is some silence around you—listen to it. That means just notice it. Pay attention to it. Listening to silence awakens the dimension of stillness within yourself, because it is only through stillness that you can be aware of silence.
—Eckhart Tolle

When the Lord wishes to draw a soul to himself, he leads it into solitude, far from the embarrassment of the world and intercourse with men, and there speaks to it with words of fire. The words of God are said to be of fire, because they melt a soul. . . In fact, they prepare the soul to submit readily to the direction of God.
—Saint Alphonsus Liguori

Barriers are sundered, fetters are melted
By the divine fire,
And the eternal dawn of a new life rises,
In all, and all in One.
—Vladimir Solovyov

Solitude and prayer are the greatest means to acquire virtues.
Purifying the mind, they make it possible to see the unseen.
Solitude, prayer, love, and abstinence are the four wheels of
the vehicle that carries our spirit heavenward.
—Saint Seraphim of Sarov

I personally became aware of the power of silence, and then eventually learned the important lesson that silence must be discovered, experienced, and then embraced, through a series of seemingly unrelated events.

The first encounter occurred when I was a very young man, about thirteen years old. I remember the day of discovery as a beautiful snowy winter morning in my home state of Michigan. For some reason I woke up earlier than the rest of the family and determined to get dressed in my winter clothing and venture outside. Behind our house there was a wooded area and I immediately headed into the woods, into a special place within the woods that I had previously identified as a place of safety and comfort. It was a place, a clearing within the woods, which always provided me with a sense of being alone, even though in reality I was surrounded by the city and the houses that made up our particular subdivision. When I arrived at the clearing that marked the space I was confronted with the crispness, the whiteness, but most of all by the silence of the place.

I don't consider myself to have been a particularly religious boy—that came much later in life—however I was raised in a believing and traditional Catholic family. Our family was faithful to attendance at Mass and the other devotions, and that life experience probably contributed to my interpretation and perception that morning, but, like any other teenage boy, I know I also had other concerns and desires at the time. I think I would have been more easily attracted by other thoughts, feelings, and emotions more readily than I would have been by silence, but yet it was the silence that captured my attention and my imagination that particular day.

I remember standing in the wooded clearing and becoming centered and focused on the experience of the silence. I found myself wondering to myself how there could be so much beauty, so much whiteness, and so wonderful of a silence in this place. I also discovered myself relating this experience to my personal understanding of who God might be and I felt a dramatic tugging, almost an invitation if you will, a desire to somehow be in a more personal encounter with this God. The experience lasted for quite a long time, but eventually the combination of the cold and the fact that I had not yet eaten my breakfast forced me to break the connection and return home. It was not until years later that I recalled and contemplated this first encounter with silence again.

A second experience, entirely unrelated to the first, occurred almost ten years later. On this occasion I found myself in the seminary chapel attending a celebration of the Eucharist. In my experience the attendance at the Eucharist was a daily event, something not at all out of the ordinary, but on this particular day, immediately after the reception of Holy Communion, I found myself back in the place of intimate silence that I had first experienced in the clearing in the woods. The experience was unannounced, unexpected, but nevertheless profound.

Although all sorts of activity surrounded me—the coming and going of the other seminarians to their assigned places for example—I was somehow able to remain focused on the experience of silence within me and not become distracted by the activity. When the Eucharist concluded and the people began to slowly leave the chapel I retained a desire to remain in my place and the experience of the intimate silence continued and deepened.

In this encounter, because my religious training was a little more intense at this point in my life, I found myself relating the experience to a scriptural reference. I prayed the words of the Apostle Peter as it is recorded in the gospel, "Lord, it is good for us to be here" (Mt 17:14). And it was good to be in the silence, it was very good.

Eventually, after the passage of a significant amount of time, I slowly felt myself leaving the privileged experience of silence and becoming more aware of the sounds and other activity around me. Much to my surprise, I did not struggle or resist the movement, even though I immediately recognized a sense of loss and disappointment. After a few more moments of simply lingering to see if anything else might occur, I left my place in chapel and went back to a normal routine. I did share this encounter with my spiritual director, who unfortunately did not recognize the moment for what it was and casually dismissed it as unimportant. As a result of his untimely direction, I did not refer to the experience again for a few more years.

The third experience of intimate silence again occurred unexpectedly and without any forewarning. This time I was visiting a place of ancient Native American Indian ruins just south of the city of Phoenix, Arizona. I was with a group of friends and we were touring the area, checking out the sites. I was certainly not expecting a religious experience; it was supposed to be a vacation.

On this particular day I became separated from the group and found myself a little off the prescribed pathway, but yet still within the permissible boundaries provided for visitors to the site. I was just standing and looking around, not for anything in particular, when I became aware that the power of the moment was not to be found in the scenery, although the desert landscape is beautiful, but rather the power of the moment was in the experience of silence that had found me again. I was quickly in relationship again with the intimate and the sacred silence of the place. How quickly the voices and the distractions of this tourist site had somehow been replaced with a completely different experience.

As I remained in the silence, I also became aware that the ground that I was standing on was a sacred place. I somehow sensed, in the silence, that this place had once been a place where others had also experienced the presence of God in their lives. In a mysterious way, even though at first glance we would seem to have nothing in common, I nevertheless sensed a connection with those who had gone before me and who had also encountered the silence of the place, perhaps expected or perhaps unexpected, as was my experience.

This third encounter with sacred silence was not prolonged; it lasted just a few minutes, but it was nevertheless an experience that was dramatic and at the same time sacred in its simplicity. When, after a few minutes, I again was clearly able to hear the voices of the other tourists who were discovering the wonders of the ancient ruins, the experience began to slip away, and I did not cling to it but rather just simply observed what was happening. At the same time, I realized that I had once again discovered, not through my own efforts, but rather unexpectedly, an experience that was important, and then I understood it as an experience that was necessary on the spiritual journey. I understood it as necessary because at that point in my life I had actually arrived at a point on the journey where I was, awake enough to recognize the potential importance of what had just occurred. I had a spiritual director who was well versed in the nuances of the spiritual journey and that encounter was not dismissed but was rather mined for all that it could provide.

I believe that I have been blessed because these three distinct encounters with silence occurred when I was least expecting it. I have been blessed because I believe I was led to a point where I understood that in the encounter with silence, the invitation to be part of the experience was profoundly present, while at the same moment I understood that it could not be controlled, or for that matter even predicted. I understood that I could embrace the experience, not in the sense of clinging to it, or packaging it, defining it or whatever, but rather to accept it as a gift, a nourishing and sacred gift that somehow sustained me in a manner that I could not completely understand but yet, at the same time, sense that it was essential and life giving.

The necessity of silence and the solitude that supports the experience may be discovered in the unexpected and in the freely given manner that I just explained. I am personally amazed at how often people in all walks of life have encountered this kind of experience, and for whom it is a powerful and sometimes even defining moment. I am perhaps even more amazed at how many times it is experienced in the lives of people and is unfortunately misunderstood, not trusted, or simply ignored. The spiritual and the sacred surround us.

As wonderful as it is to have an experience of the intimate and sacred silence come when you least expect it, more often than not the encounter with silence is not a surprise, but perhaps more accurately understood as something that is discovered as a continuing step on the spiritual journey.

As a person emerges from the experience of "intoxication," from the experience of needing to consume as many new ideas and encounters as possible, and as they celebrate the encounter with the sacred, the Other, they begin to recognize that everything that they have been wildly collecting and experiencing is in fact a distraction. It is not in the accumulation of ideas, knowledge, or even experience where God is profoundly encountered. But rather it is in the silence and the solitude, the uncluttered moment and the intimate and the sacred absence of those things that we think we need and which have been important to us.

A favorite story from the Hebrew scriptures might be both helpful and illustrative at this point. The story tells of the prophet Elijah's encounter with God, what we might today understand as a mystical experience:

"Go out and stand on the mountain before the Lord, for the Lord is about to pass by." Now there was a great wind, so strong that is was splitting mountains and breaking rocks in pieces before the Lord, but the Lord was not in the wind; and after the wind an earthquake, but the Lord was not in the earthquake; and after the earthquake a fire, but the Lord was not in the fire; and after the fire a sound of sheer silence. When Elijah heard it, he wrapped his face in his mantle and went out and stood at the entrance of the cave.

(1 Kgs 19:11–13)

Elijah, perhaps because he was a prophet and well versed in the ways of God, or perhaps because he just sensed it, understood that his encounter with God would take place in the silence, the place where any tiny whispering sound could be distinguished. The heavy winds and the crushing rocks were dramatic, as was the earthquake no doubt, but it was in the stillness after the dramatic where the encounter occurred.

Retreat centers traditionally stress silence and expect it as a necessary condition of the retreat. At times the silence may be limited to certain times during the retreat, but at other times it is not a limited silence but rather something that permeates and informs the entire experience. With the exception of the moments where there might be some kind of input from a retreat director, or shared and communal prayer, the greater portion of the time is spent in silence. Tradition plays an important role in determining the condition of silence, but perhaps even more important than tradition might be the desire of the retreat director to help the people on retreat discover for themselves the power of

51

silence, to experience what sacred silence has to offer, and finally to help the retreatants embrace the silence as the essential component of their spiritual journey.

Silence invites us to learn, to make the necessary connections in life, and perhaps ultimately it is the condition that is necessary in order to become aware of the ultimate truths of life and relationship.

Silence—as it is discovered, experienced again and again for longer periods of time, and then finally embraced as a person embraces another person whom they love, not wishing them to depart—prepares the person to enter fully into the relationship with the Other. It is recognized and understood, much as the prophet Elijah recognized and understood it in his encounter with the Other, as the necessary space that is required for communication, discovery, growth in the acquired skill of awareness, and even further awakening. Silence leads to a way of living life that can best be described as contemplative.

Although there are many different definitions that are used to define the meaning of contemplation, I prefer to understand it as soul food, the essential nutrient that fuels the spirit of the human person, enabling the intimate response to the Other. Without the experience of contemplation, any response to the Other would be incomplete, unfulfilling, and ultimately lead a person further away from the experience of intimacy rather than becoming fully engaged in the relationship.

As I stood in the clearing in the woods so many years ago, I did not realize that I was being nourished. When I was invited into the ultimate silence and connection with the Other while in the seminary chapel or when visiting the ruins outside of Phoenix, I did not yet understand the necessity of the experience. A good and wise retreat director, a retreat facility staff that understands the connection between silence and the experience of God, will help a person make the connection and understand what may be required next.

CHAPTER SIX

CONVERSION: A CHANGE IN ATTITUDE AND PERCEPTION

Go ahead light your candles and burn your incense and ring your bells and call out to God, but watch out, because God will come and he will put you on his anvil and fire up his forge and beat you and beat you until he turns brass into pure gold.
—Sant Keshavadas

Every authentic religious epiphany or encounter, every true experience of God, in whatever form, makes a person less insular, less complacent, and less isolated—and more restless, more inspired and more engaged with the world and humanity.
—Anthony Gittins

These perspectives will appear absurd to those who don't see that life is, from its origins, groping, adventurous, and dangerous. But these perspectives will grow, like an irresistible idea on the horizon of new generations.
—Teilhard de Chardin

The experience of conversion—understood in the spiritual sense as the call to change, to repent, or to embrace a new way of living—is a dominant theme throughout the Bible. The prophets of the Hebrew scriptures often challenged the people of Israel to change their ways, to abandon one type of living and to embrace another type of living that would be more in line with the prophet's understanding of what was essential and necessary for the people of the covenant. The call to repent, to see and hear things the way that the Lord sees and hears things, is made by prophet Isaiah: "Listen, you deaf! Look and see you blind! . . . You have seen many things but not observed them; your ears are open but you do not hear" (Is 42: 18, 20, *Revised Standard Version*).

In the Christian scriptures the constant refrain from John the Baptist, "Prepare the way of the Lord, make straight his paths" (Mt. 3:3), picked up the old prophetic theme of change and repentance with an added a twist. John required a ritual baptism with water in response to the reception of his message that acknowledged sinfulness in the individual life of the person who responded. Jesus expanded upon the message of the Baptist when he preached early in his ministry, "Repent, for the kingdom of heaven has come near" (Mt 4:17). The message of Jesus, in contrast with John, did not require a ritual action in response but rather offered a reason and a vision, both of which were understood in his teaching about the kingdom of heaven by the people who responded to this call.

In the Christian tradition, influenced by consistent preaching over the last two thousand years about the need to convert and change one's life, the idea of conversion has perhaps become a loaded word when used in a spiritual context. It is not necessarily the word itself, nor for that matter the value that it proclaims, but there is something in the experience that may not initially attract us. For example, we usually don't react too strongly to the idea of conversion when we use it in reference to cooking, converting tablespoons of a specific ingredient into cups or pints. We also don't usually react too strongly when we use the term in reference to money, converting dollars to pounds or to euro for example. However, when it is used in reference to spirituality, it often produces a very different reaction. The process is not necessarily welcomed, but it rather seen as something that should be avoided if possible.

So very often when people hear the word conversion, and the concept introduced, it can be easily associated with a specific action or activity in their lives that is perceived as somehow displeasing to another person, for example the spiritual authority that is using it. When the word conversion is used most people automatically assume that they will be challenged with a perceived need, at least on the part of the person who is challenging them, to change something about their lifestyle, an opinion, or perhaps a specific action or activity. Often the call to change produces feelings of guilt, incompleteness, or even, at times, a feeling of inadequacy and discouragement.

This perception is understandable given the long history and practice of the experience. But at the same time, it is also unfortunate. Conversion as a root spiritual value has very little to do with changing a specific action or activity, but rather has everything to do with changing an attitude and perception. To emphasize the action or the activity in a very real sense distracts the person from the core value that could be embraced and enjoyed. It is really a matter of understanding and appreciating where the emphasis is to be placed, and if the emphasis is misplaced, it is often a mistake that can lead to even more frustration instead of to the integration and fullness of life, which is the intent of the conversion process and experience.

A powerful story from the life of Jesus may illustrate this point and clarify the difference. Traditionally understood as the story of the "good thief," it is related to us in the gospel of Luke, at the moment in the life of Jesus as he hangs upon the cross:

> One of the criminals who were hanged there kept deriding him and saying, "Are you not the Messiah? Save yourself and us!" But the other rebuked him, saying, "Do you not fear God, since you are under the same sentence of condemnation? And we indeed have been condemned justly, for we are getting what we deserve for our deeds, but this man has done nothing wrong." Then he said, "Jesus, remember me when you come into your kingdom." He replied, "Truly I tell you, today you will be with me in Paradise."
>
> **(Lk 23:39–43)**

More often than not, the emphasis given to the story is on the action of the designated "good thief" in contrast to the "bad thief." From a certain well established perspective and interpretation, the good thief acknowledges sin, accepts his condemnation, and is aware of the fact that God will soon have something to say about all of this, since his death and final judgment seem to be imminent. The bad thief, on the other hand, shows little acknowledgement or acceptance of what is happening and persists in his "bad" behavior. In the traditional and perhaps even comfortable interpretation of the story, Jesus saves the good thief because he repents, and we assume, the bad thief is not saved since he does not repent. There is often a feeling of some sort of satisfaction when we hear and interpret the story in this way, and it does fit into our concept of what conversion might be about. The good thief converts, even if it is at the last moment.

But what happens if the story is not about the action or inaction of either one of the thieves? What happens to our understanding and appreciation of the story if the story is not about conversion in the way that we might understand it but is rather a story about the generosity of God? What happens if conversion is more about generosity than it is about repentance or even justice? Viewed in this sense the story is about Jesus, a wise, generous, loving, and forgiving man, who even at the point of his own death continues to be wise, generous, loving, and forgiving. From the Christian perspective Jesus is all of this because Jesus is God and represents, even to the last, the Abba God of which he invited people to be in relationship with, the Abba God of the promised kingdom of God.

If the story is really about the generosity of God, is there anything in the story that we can learn about conversion? The answer is yes, but the emphasis is not on the action of either the good thief or the bad thief. The lesson is presented to us, but in order for the lesson to be learned we are required to view the story in a different way.

Perhaps the story suggests that conversion is not so much an action but is rather an attitude, a perception of life that so permeates the vision and understanding of a person that it permits the most generous and the most surprising reaction possible, even in moments of great trauma and personal suffering. Jesus, who even at the last moment of his life continues to inspire his disciples with his vision of the kingdom of God, models the converted attitude that the story intends to teach. Understood in this sense perhaps a converted person, who has learned from Jesus that which is required, would turn their attention, not to the "good thief" who is promised heaven, but rather to the "bad thief" who seemingly has lost everything with the question, "What generous, loving, and forgiving thing is God going to do for him?"

Conversion is not about action and activity, although a converted person will try and live a life where their personal actions and activities represent a significant change of perception and focus. Conversion is rather an attitude, it is a way of seeing and understanding life that then permeates and animates the choices and the decisions that we daily make. As a result of embracing this new attitude as a defining and essential stance in life, a working definition of conversion might emphasize not only the need to repent and to have a change of heart but also the need to "see as God sees" and to be as "generous as God is generous."

Conversion is the point where the skills that we have practiced—awareness, awakening, silence, and solitude—all converge. Conversion is the result of becoming aware and awake, of looking at the "big picture," resisting the urge to be narrowly focused, convinced of our own limited opinions and judgments. Conversion takes place in the silence and the solitude, the place where we encounter God, the Other, and where we understand and accept that it is "not our way, but God's way." Another story, a parable from the life of Jesus, further illustrates the point.

In chapter twenty of the gospel of Matthew, we are told the story about the owner of a vineyard who goes out at all hours of the day to hire workers who will work in the vineyard. He goes out early in the morning, at mid-morning, at noon, at mid-afternoon, and finally he even goes out immediately before the end of the workday. In each instance he finds workers who are in need of a job and he sends them all to go and work in his vineyard.

When it comes time for payment, the owner of the vineyard informs his steward to pay each person, beginning with the last person hired, the standard and agreed upon sum for a full day of labor. When the workers who were hired first, and who worked all day, observed that the workers who labored for only a short period of time were paid a full day's wage, they assumed that they would be getting more. But they did not, and as a result of receiving an amount that they perceived to be unjust, complained to the owner of the vineyard. His response to their complaint: "Do I not have the right to be generous?"

Traditionally when we hear this story we assume that this is a story about the generosity of God. And, of course, in one sense it is a story about the generosity of God. But might it also be a story about conversion? Might it also be one of the stories that Jesus used to teach his apostles and his disciples about the necessary attitude and perception of a person who lived in the kingdom of God? Understood in this way it is a story where Jesus challenges his followers to identify with the person who worked all day in the vineyard, but not to imitate them. It is a story where he challenges his followers to convert their attitude: Instead of complaining about the generosity of God and somehow feeling shortchanged, rejoice that others received the generosity of God, and rejoice that you were a witness to it, even if it means that you had to work very hard all day for exactly the same wage.

It is this converted attitude and perception that truly animates a person who seeks to live in the kingdom of God that Jesus preached. It is this converted attitude that helps a person understand some of the other teachings of Jesus. "'Lord, if another member of the church sins against me, how often should I forgive? As many as seven times?' Jesus said to him, 'Not seven times, but, I tell you, seventy-seven times'" (Mt 18:21–22). Or, in another place, "For those who want to save their life will lose it, and those who lose their life for my sake will find it. For what will it profit them if they gain the whole world but forfeit their life?" (Mt 16:25–26). In each instance the challenge given to his followers is to convert an existing attitude into a new way of seeing and believing. For many people in the time of Jesus, this message was a message that they enthusiastically embraced, for still others it was very difficult. The same dynamic is at work today, two thousand years after the historical event.

If the Christian scriptures provide examples about the true meaning of conversion and the generosity of God, the scriptures also provide examples that illustrate the dynamic when the message was not well received. Perhaps one of the most profound stories about conversion in the Christian scriptures, in this example a story about a conversion that did not occur, is discovered in the story about the rich young man.

A certain ruler asked him, "Good Teacher, what must I do to inherit eternal life?" Jesus said to him, "Why do you call me good? No one is good but God alone. You know the commandments: 'You shall not commit adultery; You shall not murder; You shall not steal; You shall not bear false witness; Honor your father and mother.'" He replied, "I have kept all these since my youth." When Jesus heard this, he said to him, "There is still one thing lacking. Sell all that you own and distribute the money to the poor, and you will have treasure in heaven; then come, follow me." But when he heard this, he became sad; for he was very rich. Jesus looked at him and said, "How hard it is for those who have wealth to enter the kingdom of God! Indeed, it is easier for a camel to go through the eye of a needle than for someone who is rich to enter the kingdom of God."

(Lk 18: 18–25)

In this story the man is presented as a person who lives a very moral and upright life. He follows all of the commandments and tries his best to follow the will of God as he understands it. Jesus recognizes his basic goodness and challenges him to conversion, to change his way of seeing.

At first we might assume that he had no reason to convert, none of his actions seemed out of place, but the call to conversion was not a call to change his actions, but rather to change his attitude and his perception of life, to change his heart. And as the story tells us, this man was unable to make the change; he was unable to convert, to accept the invitation that Jesus presented him.

The rich young man in the story is not a bad person. The rich young man in the story is a person who is spiritual and who is trying to live an upright and blessed life. At the same time it may be assumed that despite his goodness, despite his efforts, there was still something missing.

In the silence and in the solitude of prayer, through the guidance of the Spirit of God, we are invited to the experience of conversion. Some of our perceptions, attitudes, and judgments will easily be converted while still others, especially those that we might believe define our personalities or which might be of the greatest importance to us, may take a little longer.

Although the conversion process is a very personal process, it is nevertheless a process that can be engaged in not only with the grace of God at work, but also with the help of a spiritual mentor or director. A person who is engaged in a retreat experience might discover that the direction and the life experience of the retreat director may be very beneficial. A retreat director cannot perform the necessary work that is involved in the conversion process—that will be your personal response to the activity and the invitation of God in your life—but a director can provide you with some help, encouragement, and join you in prayer. The retreat director can also be a person who helps to sustain and encourage you as you learn to see in a new way, to respond to the world around you with a converted attitude of generosity.

CHAPTER **SEVEN**

THE ABUNDANT LIFE

The Great Way is not difficult for those who do not pick and choose. When preferences are cast aside the Way stands clear and undisguised. But even slight distinctions made set earth and heaven far apart.
—Seng-ts'an

We should not prefer power to weakness, nor prefer health to sickness, wealth to poverty, pleasure to pain, this work to that one, and so it is with all things.
—Saint Ignatius of Loyola

All things speak of God to those who know Him, and because they reveal Him to all those who love Him, these same things hide Him from those who do not know Him.
—Blaise Pascal

I begged for power and found it in knowledge. I begged for honor and found it in poverty. I begged for health and found it is asceticism. I begged my account be lessened before God and found it in silence. I begged for consolation and found it in despair.
—Ali Sahl Isfahani

Earth's crammed with heaven,
And every common bush afire with God;
But only he who sees, takes off his shoes.
—Elizabeth Barrett Browning, *"Aurora Leigh"*

We are not human beings having a spiritual experience.
We are spiritual beings having a human experience.
—Teilhard de Chardin

Two swimming pools, side by side, may provide a helpful image for our concluding reflection. One pool, the pool we might recognize as designated for the very young, is the wading pool. The deepest part of this pool does not exceed the depth of one foot. Next to the wading pool, or at least very close to the pool, is the pool that is intended for adults, those who are able to swim. The depths of this pool might begin at three feet but the depth dramatically increases to provide an opportunity for diving or, for that matter, just peacefully floating and bobbing.

As you observe each of the pools you will notice all sorts of activity. Some people will be splashing and swimming, having a wonderful time. Still others might be sitting on the side of the pool, just soaking their feet in the clear and inviting water. Some people will be diving, while still others might be in the deepest part of the pool, exploring the bottom of the pool for hidden treasures or perhaps a coin that has been lost. At first glance the activity seems to be quite similar, and we can certainly assert that in each instance the people using either pool are in fact "swimming," but there is a huge difference between swimming in a wading pool and swimming in a pool that is much deeper.

If you permit each of the pools to symbolize the spiritual journey and perspective on life of an individual person, there will be stark differences. It would not be too much of a stretch of the imagination to assume that each person's perceptions, opinions, and judgments about what it means to swim will not be the same. Although people share a common experience and there will necessarily be points of contact, at the same time there will be even more points of divergence.

A person whose experience of life and whose perception of life is symbolized by the wading pool may well be a person who is expending all sorts of energy and who is seemingly fully engaged in what he is doing. However, because the depth of the pool is not deep, such a person may also be persuaded to believe certain things about life which are true from that perspective but which are in fact extremely limiting and not at all necessary. When your perspective seems to suggest that there is only a limited amount of a specific resource available to you, in this instance water, you may strongly believe that it needs to be measured, controlled, and parceled out. There is a potential scarcity of the resource just over the horizon.

A person whose experience of life and whose perception of life are symbolized by the pool that is very deep will see and experience life in a completely different manner. With this experience, such a person, because of their experience, will not be easily persuaded that the important resources in life need to be measured, controlled, or parceled out. For this person life is the experience of abundance and of possibility.

Spiritual masters from all different traditions model and teach the truth about the abundant life, or perhaps another way of looking at it, a life of limitless possibilities. Again and again we are reminded that it is our perceptions, the judgments and the opinions that we form as a result of these perceptions, which can lead us to a false understanding, or illusion, "now we see in a mirror dimly," (1 Cor 13:12). On the other hand if we embrace the process of growing in awareness daily, celebrate our awakened self, seek out silence and solitude, and permit the spirit of God to mold us and change us, our vision will be much improved.

In the chapter fourteen of the gospel of Matthew, we discover a powerful story that can illustrate the difference between scarcity and abundance. It is a powerful story about changing your perception and learning to see the way that God sees.

The apostles come to Jesus and point out the obvious: It is the dinner hour and the people who have gathered to listen to him are hungry. The apostles also report to Jesus that they have calculated the numbers and completed the math: There are five thousand people and all the food that they can rustle up in this enormous crowd is five loaves and two fish. In other words the apostles report to Jesus that there is not enough, there is a scarcity of what the people need. Jesus looks around and sees something completely different. He sees that there is "more than enough," that there is an abundance of all that is required. Jesus responds to the report of scarcity related to him by his apostles by telling the people to sit down, by blessing that which the apostles have given him, and then inviting all to share what has been blessed. The abundance has been revealed. Not only is there enough to feed the five thousand, there is more than enough left over to feed even more. The people have been freed by Jesus from their fear and their anxiety, and because they have been freed, they now enjoy the abundance which had been in their midst from the very start but which they were unable to see.

So very often when this story is retold and interpreted the emphasis is on the miraculous, the miracle that Jesus performs. Although it is certainly an accurate interpretation of the story, perhaps the miracle is in the revelation of the ordinary, and not necessarily the emphasis on the extraordinary. If the emphasis is on the extraordinary, the miracle performed by Jesus, it then seems as something that is entirely out of the realm of possibility for ordinary people. If, on the other hand, the emphasis is on the ordinary, not so much miraculous power but rather the power that comes from learning to see in a new way, then the event is not simply a wonderful memory of what Jesus did, but an experience that can be enjoyed and celebrated in our own time and place.

The story powerfully illustrates the power of perception. The story demonstrates the profound difference between the ability to recognize the abundance that is present rather than to see only the scarcity or the lack of something that is essential. In the one instance, the viewpoint modeled for us by Jesus, we are presented with his vision of life, a vision which recognizes that all that is needed is available to us. In the second instance, modeled for us by the apostles and the crowd, there is a working presumption and acceptance that something is missing, or at the very least, in very short supply.

What Jesus models for us in this story and in the example of his life, is so profoundly different and in contrast to what seems to be the lived experience of many, that it may seem to be impossible. However, acknowledging the seemingly impossible, perhaps if we are willing to let our imagination run wild, if just for a moment, we might recognize that it could be possible and that the extraordinary experience of life could be the ordinary experience of life. Once we give ourselves permission to imagine and even believe, perhaps we might then recognize in the possibility an experience of what Jesus identified as the kingdom of God and that we might yet learn to recognize is in our midst.

That being said there can nevertheless be a response and acceptance of the kingdom of God, a daily living of the Kingdom, that is not dependent on the many, the crowd, or all of the people, but also as a personal decision in life. An individual person, moving in response to the power of grace through the essential steps on the spiritual path, can experience the abundance of God and reject a vision of life that sees only what is lacking, or in short supply. The key may be found not only in perception, but also in perseverance on the spiritual path, and in the language that we use to describe our experience.

The language of scarcity is a language and an experience of life that is based on conditions, shoulds, fears, anxieties, doubts, and the like. It is a language and an experience in life that has at its root the condition that all needs to be protected, measured, and parceled out to ensure that you will not run out. It is a language that will not give an inch, will never presume innocence, does not believe in forgiveness ("How often should I forgive? As many as seven times?"), demands justice, and is never satisfied, filled, or completed. It is a language and a way of life that is based on the conviction that there is never enough, and what little bit you may have might not be enough.

The language of abundance, on the other hand, is a language and an experience of life that is grounded in the belief that God is filled with plenty. It is the experience of invitation, encouragement, confidence, gratefulness, and generosity. It is a language and an experience in life that has at its core the belief that love gives life, that forgiveness generates hope ("Not seven times, but I tell you, seventy-seven times"), and that all will be completed, accomplished, and fulfilled according to the plan of God, "not what I want but what you want" (Mt 26:39).

We end where we began, on the windswept plains with our ancestor in faith, Abraham. As Abraham learned and progressed on his spiritual path, as he experienced the movement from awareness to awakening in his encounters with the Other whom he learned to recognize as God, and in the events and the experiences of his life that brought him to a new way of seeing, Abraham eventually encountered the way of abundance and limitless possibilities. The vision is recorded for us in the book of Genesis:

But the word of the Lord came to him . . . He brought him outside and said, "Look toward heaven and count the stars, if you are able to count them." Then he said to him, "So shall your descendants be." And he believed the Lord; and the Lord reckoned it to him as righteousness. Then he said to him, "I am the Lord who brought you from Ur of the Chaldeans, to give you this land to possess."
(Gn 15:4–7)

For Abraham the experience of the abundant life was symbolized by the promise of unlimited descendents and the richest land for grazing and living imaginable. It is the experience of abundance that would certainly appeal to a Bedouin nomad, although not necessarily to a person with modern sensibilities. Nevertheless it is dramatic in its simplicity.

Perhaps today, for a person who lives in a consumer-driven culture where we are surrounded with a myriad of choices and options, the promise of the abundance of another "thing" or "more stuff" will not capture our imagination or even animate and inspire us. But the promise of living a life that is not burdened down, a life that enables us to see with clarity of vision and purpose, a life that integrates instead of separates, that may well appeal to us. In the experience of the Other, in the experience of daily life in the kingdom of God, it becomes a reality for all those who accept the invitation to seek and to learn a new way.

PART TWO:

How?

CHAPTER EIGHT

RETREATS PAST AND PRESENT

Saint Ignatius confessed one day to Father Laynez that a single hour of meditation at Manresa had taught him more truths about heavenly things than all the teachings of all the doctors put together could have taught him. On (one) occasion his spirit was ravished in God . . . this last vision flooded his heart with such sweetness, that the mere memory of it in aftertimes made him shed abundant tears.
—David Cooper,
***Silence, Simplicity, and Solitude* (Skylight Paths, 1999)**

In every movement God is present since it is impossible to make any move or utter a word without the might of God.
—Dov Baer of Mezhirich

I n the sixteenth century a young and aristocratic man from Spain chose to do what young and aristocratic men of his time routinely discerned was required of them. He went off to war in one of the almost non-stop battles of the day between conflicting noble families. It is really of little importance to note that the battle was at the citadel of

Pampeluna, or that the principals who were fighting, in this case it was the Spanish and the French, or that the date was May 20, 1521; in a very real sense all of that information is secondary to our story.

The young man, known today as Saint Ignatius of Loyola (1491–1556), the founder of the Society of Jesus, generally called the Jesuits, may have been caught up in the excitement of the cause, but he was not very lucky in the ways of war. Ignatius was wounded quickly, carried from the battlefield, and sent off to a quiet place to recuperate and mend his wounds. While in this infirm state, when the pain subsided enough to think of other things, he became restless with his lot. In an attempt to fill the long periods of inactivity and boredom he began to read the romantic and chivalrous stories of his day, hoping to be entertained if not inspired by the stories of the great knights and their ladies. He quickly discovered the popular stories to be unsatisfactory and surprisingly unappealing. In his restlessness he desired something more. Eventually Ignatius discovered a remedy to his dilemma—and the inspiration that would fuel the rest of his life—the stories of the Christian saints and their Lord Jesus Christ.

Saint Ignatius discovered, in the time that he devoted to reading, prayer, and meditation, a deepening relationship with the person of Jesus. He recorded his progress, along with the questions that he formed and then answered, and developed a method that resulted in his own transformation and awakening. In and of itself, this method was not entirely unique. There have been others who have certainly recorded their spiritual progress in much the same way. However, what was unique was that the saint offered what he learned and experienced to others who were also interested in the spiritual life, and when they engaged in his method, they discovered that it brought them to the same kind of transformation and awareness.

At the time of his death in 1556, one thousand men had joined the Society of Jesus; remarkably each of them was trained and formed in the spiritual method of Saint Ignatius. The method of prayer, meditation, and spiritual direction, put into writing by Ignatius in his book *Spiritual Exercises* and therefore simply referred to as the Spiritual Exercises, brought people to an awareness and a commitment to the person of Jesus. But because the exercises were reflective of the spiritual journey of the saint, the exercises also bonded to the person who performed them something of the charism, the enthusiasm, and the conviction of Saint Ignatius of Loyola. The Spiritual Exercises proved to be the springboard of a formidable force for change in the lives of those who encountered them, including the vast multitude that has passed and continues to pass through the ranks of the Jesuits.

The Spiritual Exercises are generally experienced within the context of a thirty-day retreat, today routinely extended even longer with a period of days dedicated to preparation for the exercises and ending with a period of time after the retreat. For those who are unable to dedicate the necessary time for the extended retreat, another model for making the exercises over the period of a year exists and is known as the nineteenth annotation.

A crucial component of the Spiritual Exercises is the trained director who guides and leads the retreatant through the exercises. This director is skilled not only in the method of the exercises, but perhaps even more importantly commits himself or herself to the support and encouragement of the person making the exercises through dedicated prayer for the retreatant. In a very real sense, the spirit and the soul of the director and the retreatant are joined together during the time of the retreat, providing for a powerful experience of grace in action.

Another legacy of the Spiritual Exercises is that the exercises clearly focused people's attention on a method and process that enabled and encouraged spiritual growth. Until the time of Saint Ignatius, a spiritual retreat, although not unknown, was rarely a regular component of the spiritual formation process. The monastic life of monks and nuns formed them by the silence and the rhythm of the daily schedule of prayer and living. However, men and women who did live a monastic life, who lived an active life, had very little opportunity or encouragement for this kind of prayer and meditation. The members of the Society of Jesus were not monks but were rather active and public spiritual representatives, men who nevertheless were formed in a spiritual tradition and who were faithful to a spiritual practice. People noticed the difference and recognized an opportunity for their own spiritual growth.

The person who popularized the idea of a personal retreat as an essential component of the spiritual formation of an individual person was Saint Francis de Sales (1567–1622). To give some substance and perspective to his assertion, Francis appealed to the vision and the inspiration of Saint Ignatius, to numerous early fathers and mothers of the church and other ecclesiastical writers, and ultimately to the example of Jesus, who spent forty days of prayer in the desert after his baptism. However, despite the fact that he grounded the idea in the experience of others, he provided the consistent example and encouragement, not so much for clerics and monks, but for common lay men and even women (a consideration almost unheard of in his own day).

From the example of Saint Francis de Sales, other saints continued the tradition and enabled the slow and continued growth of the idea of retreats. Among these saints were Saint Vincent de Paul, who organized retreats throughout France, the venerable Catherine de Francheville, also in France but specifically for women, Saint Alphonsus Liguori in the Kingdom of Naples, who insisted that the houses of his congregation, the Redemptorists, make provisions for retreats for all who were interested, and others who established the movement throughout Europe and also in other parts of the world.

The first retreat house in the United States, erected specifically for the purpose of providing space dedicated to performing the spiritual exercises commonly associated with a retreat, was founded on Staten Island, New York in 1911. From this retreat center, and from other places in the country, the retreat movement took root and spread rapidly. By 1927 there was a retreat league established in Boston, Massachusetts, for the purpose of encouraging retreats, and by 1941 this league was also firmly established in Canada. Once established, the popularity of retreats exploded. By 1997, only eighty-six years after the first retreat house was established, over 1.2 million Catholics would go on retreat in the United States alone.

Although it can be asserted with some confidence that the retreat movement has its roots deep within the Roman Catholic tradition, other communities and organizations, representative of a variety of different faith traditions, have contributed to the continued growth and development of retreats. Today there are many different retreat and renewal centers, places of sacred refuge and places of sacred destination that can be discovered. There are Lutheran, Methodist, Baptist, Quaker, Assembly of God, Jewish, and other community and church sponsored retreat centers that serve all those who seek a retreat opportunity. The diversity of these religious traditions has enriched all who seek the experience of God.

Regardless of the faith tradition that animates the particular retreat center, there are particular types and formats that retreats tend to take. For the purpose of our reflection here it may be helpful to describe six different categories.

A *conference* or *preached* retreat is perhaps the most popular format and experience of retreat for people, especially those who are going on a retreat for the first time. In this retreat format, typically presented over a weekend, a group of people reflect on a specific topic, presented by a single speaker or occasionally a panel of speakers. A central theme is the glue that holds the group together and focuses their attention. In between the formal presentations, opportunity is provided for private prayer and reflection, liturgical activities such as communal prayer or a specific devotional practice, and of course meals and other necessities.

The central theme for a preached or conference style retreat is varied, dependent on the expertise of the presenter and the particular interest of the participants. Retreats that consider a specific Christian theme during the liturgical seasons of Lent and Advent are quite popular. Retreat centers often make a special effort to offer retreats of varying lengths and formats in the weeks that precede Christmas in the winter and Easter Sunday in the spring. Retreats that prepare people for a life change or experience, such as a retreat for those who are engaged to be married or who are preparing to accept a specific ministerial task within the community, are also popular. Still other retreats consider specific topics that may be of interest to a diverse group of people, such as a retreat considering feminine or male spirituality, perhaps a retreat learning how to use the enneagram for personal growth, or a retreat that explores a specific kind of prayer (Centering, Contemplative, the use of *Lectio Divina*, etc.).

A *guided retreat* is a variation on the conference or preached retreat format. A guided retreat usually has a smaller group of people in attendance, often no more than twenty to twenty-five, and sometimes even smaller, depending on the topic that is being presented. The presenter offers a reflection on the topic and then guides the retreatants to a further exploration of the topic, which will take place away from the communal activity of the group. Specific readings may be provided for reflection, certain scriptural texts proposed for consideration, a specific task may be suggested, but the majority of the retreat experience is generated by the response and the need of the individual person to the theme. As such it is not unusual in the guided retreat experience that the retreatant, although initially attracted to the topic under consideration, may find himself or herself laying the original topic aside, pursuing and reflecting on some other point that captured their attention and imagination.

A guided retreat often presents the opportunity for the person on retreat to meet individually with the retreat director or another spiritual director. It is also not unusual for there to be optional opportunities for group conversation on the theme to provide the retreatants with an opportunity to share their insights and experiences. The dynamic of listening to others share their progress, struggles, challenges, and joys can be very beneficial. Many times, as I have reviewed the submitted evaluations of a retreat weekend, I take note that it was not necessarily the presenter or the topic that produced the most favorable commentary, but rather the interaction between the participants who made the retreat. This serves as a wonderful corrective for the retreat director who may believe that everything depends on him or her!

A *directed retreat* in the spirit of Saint Ignatius of Loyola is traditionally an extended period of retreat, from as little as a few days to as long as thirty days. In the directed retreat format, the retreatant meets with a trained retreat director who leads them through the Spiritual Exercises as proposed by the saint. The retreatant is committed to as many as four or five formal prayer periods a day in which a specific scriptural theme is reflected upon. In addition to the formal period of prayer, the retreatant meets with their personal retreat director at least once and sometimes twice a day for a determined period of time. In the meeting with the director, the dynamic is a powerful exchange: The retreatant reports their progress and the director encourages and enables the movement of the retreatant to the point that Saint Ignatius identifies as "election" (the authentic discernment of what God is asking me to do, my vocation in life).

A directed retreat in the tradition of Saint Ignatius can be a powerful spiritual experience. Many people have completed the Spiritual Exercises and routinely define the experience as "the moment" of conversion and clarity in their life.

A *12-step retreat* based on the 12 steps of Alcoholics Anonymous is slowly emerging as a popular retreat option for many people. Twelve-step retreats can be experienced within the preached or conference style retreat format. In this format the presenter(s) speak on various points relating to sobriety, such as self-examination, making amends, or the spiritual disciplines of meditation and prayer. In a 12-step directed retreat format, group work is replaced with an individual working through the steps with a trained spiritual director. The 12-step directed retreat format usually concentrates on specific steps that the retreatant may be working on and is particularly useful in preparation for the fifth step in which the person, admits "to God, to ourselves, and to another human being the exact nature of our wrongs."

12-step retreats are increasingly the portal through which many people initially pass as they become introduced to the concept of a retreat. The attraction may at first be to work on the issues concerned with maintaining a life of sobriety. Eventually, however, the sobriety work and the deepening experience of their personal relationship with God, become interwoven. Sobriety is understood as the path to a significant relationship with God and God is understood as the person from whom the gift of sobriety is received.

A *personal retreat* is intended for people who seek time away, in solitude and silence, and who need a minimum, if any, input or direction. A person who seeks the time and the space for a personal retreat is often experienced in the ebb and flow, the particular rhythm and movement of the retreat experience. Crucial to the success of a personal retreat is the ability to be comfortable with the silence and the independence of the experience. For this reason it is very helpful, and will enhance the retreat experience, if the person has a well defined goal and expectation for their time away.

A good candidate for a personal retreat is a person who manages and disciplines their time well. A rigid schedule of the day is most certainly not a requirement, but a balance of sleeping, eating, prayer, reflection, and some sort of exercise, as simple as an extended, gentle walk, can all contribute to a powerful retreat experience.

An *extended retreat*, usually of at least eight days or more, is perhaps a luxury, and in our society and culture, almost an embarrassment of riches. But yet extended retreats are not at all uncommon as more and more people discover the truly healing power that can be experienced during this "vacation of the soul."

An extended retreat can be a preached or a conference type retreat, and in such instances the schedule of the retreat usually includes two or three periods of group reflection, or it can be a directed or guided retreat. For some people an extended retreat is completely personal, with little or no group activity, beyond attendance at common liturgical functions—the rest of the time is spent devoted to the particular rhythm that develops during the retreat.

In choosing a retreat it is important to determine and understand the format that will be used. If a person is arriving at the retreat center with the expectation that there time will be unstructured, they may want to ask for a schedule of the day in advance of their arrival. A preached or conference style retreat may not have much free time included. If, on the other hand, you are seeking structure and definition for your retreat experience, a preached or conference style retreat may be just what you are looking for. So it is with each of the different formats used for retreat. Determine what format may best meet your needs, ask the necessary questions of the retreat directors and staff, and then commit yourself to the process.

CHAPTER **NINE**

CHOOSING A
RETREAT CENTER

"Cheshire Puss," she began. . . . "Would you tell me, please, which way I ought to go from here?" "That depends a good deal on where you want to get to," said the Cat. "I don't much care where—" said Alice. "Then it doesn't matter which way you go," said the Cat. "—so long as I get SOMEWHERE," Alice added as an explanation. "Oh, you're sure to do that," said the Cat, " if you only walk long enough."
—**Lewis Carroll,** *Alice's Adventures in Wonderland*

People find it difficult to understand why one must travel to the master in order to hear the teaching from his lips because, as they see it, one can study moralistic works. But this is of great value, for there is a great difference between hearing the truth from the master directly, and hearing it quoted by others in his name
—**Nahman of Bratslav**

If you have become intrigued by the idea of exploring your inner self as a spiritual person or making some kind of tentative step to learn more about your personal relationship with God; if your imagination has been captured by the idea of something that can be appreciated and understood as both new and at the same time traditional; if a previously unidentified or unexplored thought or feeling begins to focus your attention on the idea of visiting a place of spiritual growth and renewal; if any of this is true, you may well be ready for the experience of making a retreat.

For many people the discovery of a sacred refuge, a place that attends to the needs of the spirit and helps them grow in awareness as a spiritual person, eventually becomes an essential part of their life. For some people the experience of a retreat becomes part of their routine, fully integrated and balanced with all of the other choices and the decisions that must be made. For still others a retreat becomes a special opportunity, an experience that cannot be routinely repeated but which is understood as an option, to be utilized when the need arises. These perspectives are helpful reflections when you begin the process of choosing a place for your retreat experience.

The first place to begin, and more often than not the first choice of a person when they engage the process of exploring possibilities, is to determine the options that are available in the local neighborhood or city. There are very few population centers in North America that are not in convenient proximity to a retreat center, abbey, house of prayer, hermitage, or some other place that has been set apart and designed for prayer and reflection. Not every person will have a center for spirituality within walking distance, although in some major cities this is not out of the realm of possibility. But almost everyone is at least within easy driving distance of such a place. Like many things in life, the best place to start you search for the right retreat is the people around you, your family, friends, coworkers, and fellow churchgoers or church leaders you may know. These are the people you know the best and are comfortable with, and there is a good chance that if they enjoyed a particular retreat or retreat center, so will you. However, the more options you find, the more likely you are to be satisfied with your final choice. Your local phone book is a good place to expand search. Yellow page headings that will usually produce the results you are looking for will include: retreat facilities, conference centers, holistic practitioners and centers, and other listings grouped under a church or community service organization.

Especially if you wish to widen your search even further or if you are looking for a specific type of retreat center, the next resource to check is the World Wide Web. The Internet provides many links to Web sites that specialize in retreats, spirituality and related topics. Ten of my favorite Web sites have been provided in this book (see page 141) and each of these sites will link you to even more sites that might be beneficial and set you on your way.

Your local bookstore and public library can also be a wonderful information source in your research. The magazine rack of some of the larger bookstore chains, as well as bookstores that specialize in books of spiritual and religious interest, usually display a variety of magazines that feature classified advertising for retreat and renewal centers. Your public library often provides subscription services to the most popular magazines requested by their patrons and can be easily referenced. As a general rule, magazines that are interested in holistic living, spiritual topics, massage, vegetarian living, or even regional magazines that highlight the interests and the style of living in that particular part of the country are all potential helpful resources.

As you define and narrow your search, the location of the retreat center likely will emerge as an important consideration. If you are primarily interested in easy accessibility, and if you envision participating in a retreat program that might meet weekly or monthly, for example, then proximity to your home probably is the most important variable in your final decision. If, on the other hand, proximity to your residence is not a prime consideration, other possibilities suggest themselves.

If you have resources of time and money available for your use, and are not necessarily constrained by your current obligations or circumstances, the option of choosing to travel a distance to the retreat center of your choice opens up. Planning, securing the necessary time away from work and family, the experience of travel, and the excitement at arriving at a new or a favorite destination can all contribute positively to the retreat experience. Sometimes the greater the effort and the more difficult the planning, the better the experience, because you are already significantly invested in the end result.

Specific geographic settings, for example the desert, an ocean-side beach, a hermitage in a secluded woods, or a mountain lodge, also plays an important role in setting the mood and the atmosphere of the retreat experience. Although all retreat centers place an important emphasis on certain qualities such as silence, cleanliness, simplicity, hospitality, and healthy and nutritious food, there are some elements that are nevertheless dependent on where the center is located. Or, as realtors are often fond of repeating when discussing the three most essential qualities of real estate, "location, location, and location."

A retreat center that is situated in a large metropolitan city may appeal to you as a wonderful place of sacred refuge, and there are many such places available. However, there will be restrictions and challenges dictated by city living that will need to be navigated such as parking, perhaps at an additional charge, or limited secure and protected space for walking and exercise. A retreat center located away from the metropolitan center and in a rural setting will have its definite appeal but there are also certain expectations that may be a challenge: There may not be public transportation to the center, there may be no convenient pharmacies close by, or perhaps no general store easily accessible to pick up something not packed at the last moment. In contrast all of these components are more than likely at your fingertips in a metropolitan center. In and of themselves each of these points is not an insurmountable obstacle but rather a consideration that may become important, especially if you are a distance from home or intend to remain on retreat for an extended period of time.

The weather that you can expect to encounter during your stay may also be an important consideration. If you are attending a retreat program for a few short days, weather is important but should not be the significant determinate when making your choice. Certainly everyone would prefer perfect weather while on retreat, but it is not essential. On the other hand, if you choose to be in residence at the center for an extended period of time, the weather can make a larger difference. If you are snowed in, it rains every day, the hurricane season is in full swing, or the heat is unbearable and makes it difficult to leave your room, each of these experiences have the potential to substantially impact the retreat experience and become a very important consideration.

The retreat facility itself can contribute positively or negatively to your experience. Often it is the facility that influences the perception of the retreat guest more than any other component, even more than the content of the program or the usefulness of the presentations. If the assigned room is too small, if the bed is uncomfortable, if there are not private bathrooms but rather shared bathrooms, if there is no easy chair in the room where you can comfortably sit and reflect, all of these seemingly little things, when accumulated, make a strong impression.

If you are in reasonably good health, if you have no specific physical challenges, and if you have a personal temperament that deals well with unexpected or unplanned circumstances, perhaps you may not be too concerned about the retreat facility. If, on the other hand, you know yourself to have minimum requirements in order to reach a level of personal satisfaction, it may be best to explore these requirements with the staff of the retreat center before you commit to a program or confirm a reservation. A weekend may not seem like a long time, but it can become almost unbearable if you are unable to sleep, if you cannot find anything you like to eat, or if you discover that you have to navigate long distances between the places that you are required to be in order to benefit fully from the retreat.

A consideration that is often overlooked is the age of the retreat facility: When was it constructed and what was the original purpose of the construction? As in any construction, the original intent of the builders of the facility usually defines the best use of the facility. Some facilities that are operating today as retreat centers were constructed specifically as retreat centers, while other centers were originally constructed for an entirely different purpose and later converted into a retreat facility. Sometimes the transition works very well while at other times it does not. For example, a building originally constructed to be a residence for religious women primarily engaged in teaching in a neighboring school, usually will have very large common areas and very small bedrooms. The emphasis of community life was focused on those activities that were performed in common, not necessarily in the comfort of the personal space of the resident sisters.

Even facilities that were originally constructed to function as retreat centers do not necessarily transition well to the demands and the needs of our society and culture today. Many retreat centers constructed fifty years ago, for example, were constructed with shared bathrooms, usually located between two bedrooms or sometimes situated at the end of the corridor, with one bathroom designated for the use of men and another for the use of women. Some retreat centers were constructed entirely for men or for women and this original intent dictated the construction choices that were made. A concern in summer is older buildings that have not updated with air conditioning. Needs and perceptions have changed over the years and many centers that served their clientele so well have to be updated and remodeled for effective use today.

Retreat center personnel many times prefer to see the physical challenges of their facility as adding "character," to the retreat experience. In all honesty, sometimes the added "character" is welcomed, especially if the center possesses a rich history, has a great location, or perhaps provides a spectacular view. At other times the added "character" of the center is not at all helpful and simply serves to illustrate that the facility is inadequate as a retreat center.

A final consideration might be helpful in putting this chapter into a useful perspective. Some people observe that what is ultimately important is the spiritual journey and any emphasis on comfort, accessibility, and location should be secondary. Perhaps this is true. There is a strain in some spiritual traditions that emphasizes that the path is difficult and not necessarily pleasant, and the question therefore arises: If the path is difficult should not the place where the path is pursued also mirror this truth? On the other hand, there are those who emphasize that the spiritual path has more than enough difficulty and challenges intrinsic to the journey, and there is no need to provide additional obstacles along the way. Both perspectives offer wisdom and it seems to me that the decision is a personal choice and preference.

CHAPTER **TEN**

SETTING REALISTIC GOALS AND EXPECTATIONS

What I want, my God, is that by a reversal of focus which you
alone can bring about, my terror in the face of nameless
changes destined to renew my being may be turned into an
overflowing joy at being transformed into you.
—Teilhard de Chardin

God has placed in each soul an apostle to lead us upon the
illumined path. Yet many seek life from without, unaware that it
is within them.
—Kahlil Gibran

You have determined that you will respond to the stirrings within you. You have made at least a tentative identification that these stirrings might be spiritual. You have determined that a retreat experience may well be a worthwhile investment of your time and your personal resources. You have identified specific retreat centers or other places of sacred refuge that you feel may best be able to respond to your needs. Although you have prepared well up to this point, there are still a few more steps in the process that remain. Setting realistic goals and expectations for your retreat will be very beneficial and can only contribute positively to the experience.

A first step in identifying your expectations and setting your goals is to define and place into perspective your relationship, or lack thereof, with God, no matter how you might interpret this encounter. Retreat centers, and the personnel that staff them, take seriously the experience of a personal relationship with God in the various ways that God can be encountered. (To the best of my knowledge there are no retreat centers that celebrate or promote atheism or agnosticism.) A beginning presumption of the staff and the directors of the retreat centers that you have chosen is that you share something of their same commitment and understanding of the spiritual life. In order to avoid disappointment, and to use your time at the retreat center in the best way possible, it is important to determine your starting point. Although you will not be required to discuss your relationship with God, or for that matter your lack of a relationship with God, with anyone on retreat unless you determine to do so, it is important and helpful that you know for yourself where you stand.

In order to reach a point of clarity, and identify your particular starting point, you might begin by asking yourself some basic questions. For example, is the retreat experience intended to be a chance to discover an answer to the most basic question, "Do I have a relationship with God?" Or if that is not your starting point, another question might be, "Is this retreat an opportunity for me to focus and perhaps deepen my relationship with God?" In this instance you acknowledge the experience of God in your life but feel that perhaps this relationship needs to be refreshed. There is some "catching up" that needs to be done. Yet another starting point might be best described as a question that determines the quality of the relationship: You have a defined and regular spiritual practice and discipline in place and so the retreat experience may well be a chance to learn new skills or practice skills already learned but not yet fully integrated into your entire being.

Your expectations and goals, what you expect to get out of your retreat experience, should be clear in your own mind well before you enter the doors of the retreat center. In order to avoid disappointment, it is helpful if each of your goals and expectations are as simple and as attainable as reasonably possible.

If your goal is that at the end of the retreat you will feel totally relaxed, stress free, and confident, you might be aiming too high. Perhaps a more reasonable goal is to have a certain level of satisfaction in knowing that you have taken a good first step on the spiritual path. If you expect that all of your questions about life will be answered and that you will have mastered a specific spiritual task or ritual, perhaps your expectations might need to be modified. You will eventually, and with repeated practice and attention, attain what you desire, but it will take time, and you will need to be very patient with the process. As the psalmist prays and the Second Letter of Peter restates centuries later, "a thousand years are like a day in the eyes of the Lord" (2 Pt 3:8, *Revised Standard Version*), and a retreat often brings this reality clearly into focus.

In the process of defining your expectations and goals, it is helpful to honestly access your personal openness and acceptance of defined religious and spiritual traditions: you need to know where you will fit and be the most comfortable. Your initial attraction to a specific retreat center may well have been determined because of geographical location. It is either close to where you live or it is in a place that you wish to visit. However, now that you are getting closer to making a commitment and choosing a retreat, it might be important to examine your choices again. Remember that most retreat centers are sponsored by a church or a community, rooted within their own spiritual tradition and practice. There may be certain expectations, some of which will be detailed some of which may not be detailed but rather presumed. There will also be a certain atmosphere within the center, an atmosphere created through the use of space, art, liturgical and ritual opportunities; even the menu of the dining room can make a powerful statement.

If you are a person that is most comfortable and familiar within the Christian tradition, you might consider a retreat experience that is firmly rooted in this faith tradition, at least for your first retreat experience. It can be very unsettling and even counterproductive to find yourself, for example, on retreat in a Zen center participating in a *sesshin*, when what you intended was a weekend in quiet reflection with the Christian scriptures.

Even within particular churches there can be a wide variety of retreat experiences. If you find yourself searching for truth and effective prayer practices in other religions, you may want to consider whether the retreat is going to embody a version of faith too conservative for your comfort. On the other hand, if you are looking for a traditional experience and wish to have the teachings and practices of your church emphasized and clarified, you may want to seek out a retreat more traditional in spirit.

If a speaker, or a panel of speakers, presents the retreat, it would be very important to have some idea in advance what the proposed topics under consideration are. A simple listing of the topics can be very revealing and provide you with enough insight to make an informed decision. "God's Word: My Way or the Highway," could be indicative of not only of the content of one of the presentations but also of the attitude and perception of the presenter. "Opening the Third Charka," is also very revealing. If you do not know what a *charka* is, you have some homework to do. Any time you consider a retreat outside your normal experience or particular religious tradition, you will have to decide whether an exotic and foreign situation is the retreat situation which will most benefit you. Do you want a retreat to expand your horizon with new and interesting ideas and approaches? Or do you wish to delve deeper and more richly into the traditions and modes you already use?

If the listing of the topics does not provide you with the information that you need, another resource that is helpful is to inquire if there are any materials required for the retreat. Some retreats may presume familiarity with a basic text; for example, a retreat that discusses the benefits of the enneagram might assume that you are familiar with the basic personality types that will be discussed. A retreat that requires loose fitting clothing, in basic black, with no jewelry or use of cologne or perfume, may be suggestive of extended periods of meditation in close proximity to other participants. Still other retreats—for example a retreat for married couples, a father and son retreat or a mother and daughter retreat—are intended for specific groups of people, and the content and the experience of the retreat will reflect this stated purpose.

If you are unsure or uncomfortable with any of the components of the retreat experience that you are considering attending, do not hesitate to ask the retreat center personnel to explain the specific component to you. Retreat centers and the personnel of the centers are well known for their hospitality and will be eager to clarify and explain. If, however, you receive something other than a helpful answer, or if you do not feel welcomed by the person with whom you are speaking, this might be an indication that you should perhaps look somewhere else. It is also important to remember, and very reassuring to know, that other people on the retreat also will be attending a retreat for the first time, and they too are unfamiliar with all of the elements and expectations. Your questions will enhance the experience for you and perhaps for others who may not feel as free as you do to seek the answers that are necessary.

A component that is often overlooked when choosing to participate in a retreat is the schedule of the day that you will be expected to follow. Retreat schedules are not all the same. The schedule sets the pace for the retreat and will certainly impact your experience. A particular schedule can be rather helpful and it can also be a hindrance; again it is primarily a matter of your expectations. If you are looking for specific guidance or are primarily interested in a specific topic, you may well appreciate a schedule that has some activity in session most of the time. If, on the other hand, you are looking for a minimum of input and would appreciate blocks of unscheduled time in order to process what you have heard or simply to rest and enjoy the silence, you may be more comfortable with a schedule that reflects this expectation.

In addition to the schedule that is particular to the specific retreat, retreat centers have certain scheduled events that are pretty much the same regardless of the kind of retreat you may be attending. The obvious example is meals and specified meal times, with all attendant systems and expectations. Self-serve buffet and expectations that you will clear your own table are the general rule about meals at retreat centers. Some centers may require help in the dishwashing as well. Of course buffets can only provide a limited selection of hot food. Generally this is supplemented by some selection of cold food, cereal and fruit for example. If you are a picky eater or a vegetarian, the selection on retreat will likely be somewhat limited, although many more holistic retreat centers increasingly cater to vegetarians.

Because as modern people we have become so accustomed to controlling every aspect of our environment, it is worth mentioning another element from meals that might be out of your control: the noise level, or even more troubling for some, the lack thereof. For example, in some retreat centers all meals are eaten in silence, while others might have designated places for silence and designated places for conversation. Some retreat centers eschew silence in order to play classical music or the recording of a recognized spiritual guru discussing a specific topic of interest. Perhaps most interesting can be retreat centers hosting multiple groups. While you may be there for a retreat on Ignatian spirituality, neighboring tables may play host to a raucous youth retreat (although careful retreat centers will avoid such a situation) or a more sedate course on scrapbooking. Needless to say, some make more interesting dinner fellows than others!

But just as all retreat centers have some provision for bodily nourishment, they also have something for spiritual nourishment. Common liturgical and ritual opportunities, specific to the faith tradition of the sponsor of the retreat center, are announced and the times for such gatherings are routinely posted. In a Catholic retreat center, for example, a reasonable expectation might be that there will be a daily celebration of Eucharist and specific opportunities for the celebration of the sacrament of reconciliation. If you are attending a retreat in an abbey, there will be certain times during the day when the resident community of monks will gather together in choir to sing and pray the Liturgy of the Hours. If you are attending a retreat in a house of prayer or in a hermitage you may discover that there is no common schedule and that you will be expected to set your own pace; in such a setting there may be very little common activity or communal interaction.

If you are attending a retreat that is hosted but not run by the retreat center, in other words a retreat that is not presented by a member of the resident staff because the facility has been rented to a specific group for a specific purpose, another consideration is helpful. Hosted retreats and hosted groups often bring to the retreat their own schedule of events, which may or may not compliment the normal schedule of the retreat center. The presumption of some hosted retreat groups is that you will follow their schedule and not participate in any activities of the retreat center. It is helpful to ask in advance if this will be the operating assumption.

The director of the retreat or the presenters of a specific program are the people who are ultimately responsible for determining the schedule and setting the pace of the retreat. As a general rule, I have learned that the more experienced the retreat director or presenter is, the more uncluttered a particular retreat schedule seems to be. Experienced retreat directors are comfortable with silence and inactivity, recognizing that it is in the silence and the solitude that the real work of the spirit takes place. As a general rule, and perhaps as a sweeping assumption, the less experienced a retreat director may be, the more the schedule is filled with activity.

Specific retreat programs are sometimes designed deliberately as intensive, with very little personal free time. Part of the dynamic of such programs often includes the formation of the disparate participants into a tightly-knit community at the end of the retreat. Again, if your expectations have been clearly identified and the content and the schedule of the retreat have been explained to you, you may welcome this kind of experience. On the other hand if you have not been prepared for the intensity of the experience, you may find yourself resisting the rhythm of the weekend and you will not enjoy the full benefit of the retreat. When in doubt, it is best to ask for clarification.

I recall a scene from the movie *Amadeus*. Mozart had just performed a wonderful symphony for the Emperor who was in attendance. At the end of the concert performance, Mozart excited and pleased with the result, quizzes the emperor about his reaction to what he had just heard. The emperor responds, "Too many notes, too many notes," to an obviously disappointed Mozart who believes that there was exactly the proper number of notes and not one more or less than was required. For me this story captures something of the dynamic of the retreat experience. For one person the schedule is just enough, and for another it may well be too full. It is not necessarily a question of right or wrong, but it may well have something to say about individual expectations.

A final expectation, both your expectation and the expectation of the retreat center, is some sort of financial payment for the services that you have received. The pricing policies of retreat centers are varied and there are no standardized rates, no common "rack rate" as a person might discover in a national motel or hotel. Although many retreat centers belong to national organizations that coordinate information, provide resources that are useful to the professional development of the staff, and often serve as an official spokesperson for their membership, the national organization does not set prices. There are informal surveys that are generated by the national office in which retreat centers are invited to share common information, prices, speaker fees, and other such information, which provides the administration of a retreat center with a point of reference, but that is really the extent of the service that they provide.

Generally retreat centers use one or two systems for pricing, and some retreat centers use both systems, depending on the particular retreat. The first pricing system includes a published rate for the program and usually some sort of advance deposit to be paid. In this system the expectations are clearly stated and agreed upon. A second pricing system is a little more complicated; the retreat center asks for an offering or for a donation for the services received, sometimes a "suggested offering," will be mentioned in order to provide the retreatant with a point of reference. In the offering system a person is free to match the suggested offering, increase their donation depending on their personal financial position, or for that matter offer a lesser amount than the suggested offering. Normally both pricing systems include room, board, and often even the materials that are required for the retreat.

If the retreat is hosted by the retreat center, payment for the hosted events is made directly to the sponsoring presenter or organization, and they in turn reimburse the retreat center an agreed upon amount. Again, from the point of view of the retreat center, the agreed upon price will include room and board; the personnel that are sponsoring the retreat will undoubtedly charge additional fees to cover their expenses. This is another example of the importance of clarifying, in advance, what is expected from you. If you are participating in a retreat that is hosted by the retreat center, and you are unaware that it is a hosted event, there may be a significant difference in what you are charged for the retreat and what the posted or quoted rate of the retreat center may be. On occasion I have experienced unhappy retreatants, unhappy hosts, and unhappy retreat personnel because the payment expectations had not been clearly stated and understood by each person concerned.

Some people, accustomed to bargain shopping, ask if there is any method to determine the value of the services of the retreat center, over and above personal value that they assign to the retreat experience itself. I have discovered that there is a simple formula that can be used to help a person determine if they have received a fair return for their investment. To determine the perceived value of your retreat experience, in the specific geographic location where the retreat is offered, find out what the posted and seasonal rate is, not the discounted or group rate, for a reasonably priced motel room of a national chain (Hampton Inn, Red Roof Inn, Comfort Inn), and add in the price of breakfast, lunch, and dinner at a local family style restaurant (Denny's, Perkins, Cracker Barrel). This formula will provide you with the costs associated with the basic services that you have received, although it does not take into consideration the professional services that you may also receive from the staff of the retreat center. This formula will not answer all of your questions but it may provide a point of reference and it may even surprise you; retreat centers are typically a real bargain.

CHAPTER ELEVEN

THE ROLE OF THE RETREAT DIRECTOR

It is very important that a person, desiring to advance in recollection and perfection, take care into whose hands he entrusts himself, for the disciple will become like the master, and as is the father so will be the son.
—Saint John of the Cross

It is very important that the master have prudence—I mean that he have good judgment—and experience; if besides these he has learning, so much the better. But if one cannot find these three qualifications together, the first two are more important, since men with a background in studies can be sought out and consulted when there is need.
—Saint Teresa of Avila

An extremely devout person, a Hasid, came to complain to his rabbi about two men in back of the synagogue. "Look at them, Rabbi—they are talking to each other while they are supposed to be praying." And the rabbi replied, "It's the other way around. Even while they are talking to each other, they are praying."

—Rabbi Joseph Gelberman,
Zen Judaism: Teaching Tales
(Crossing Press, 2001)

Doctor Leo Buscalia once told a story about himself that I found to be very revealing. According to the doctor, he was taking an afternoon walk through a monastery garden with a Zen master, and with some pride was describing to the master some of his ideas and theories about the formation of the human heart. Suddenly, in the midst of their walk and Leo's explanation, the Zen master turned and slapped him with the words, "Don't walk in my head with your dirty shoes!" This provides a poignant insight into the role of the retreat director.

The essential, and in my opinion non-negotiable, quality of a good retreat director is that the director must be respectful of the spiritual journey of the person who seeks their direction. The retreat director is not God, he or she is not the significant Other. The retreat director is not the person with whom the retreatant seeks to establish a relationship. The retreat director is, or at least should be, simply another person who is also walking the spiritual journey, serving as a companion on the journey with the retreatant and nothing more. The retreat director may have particular skills and talents, perhaps they may be helpful at a certain stage in the spiritual journey because they have experienced the path already taken, but the director is not an expert, and does not have the final word on all matters.

As a person who is fundamentally respectful of the spiritual journey, the retreat director must approach each encounter with the soul and spirit of another person with a profound feeling of awe and wonder, acknowledging the presence of God that is already powerfully present and at work in the lives of the people on retreat. It is not up to the retreat director to make specific judgments about the supposed quality or lack of quality that may be present in the retreatant's relationship with God. The retreat director listens to the story of faith, the story of the journey, and listens with a hungry ear, in a very real sense sharing in the nourishment that has sustained the person who is telling the story of their unique journey with God.

A retreat director should be committed to listening to what another person has to share, and be willing to gently guide and encourage a possible way to further encounter with God. In the listening there may well be times when a certain behavior or perception is shared that the director may understand as a possible obstacle to further growth and development. In such an instance, for example a person shares that he or she is currently struggling with an addictive substance or find themselves in a less than life giving relationship with a spouse or partner, the role of the director is to encourage and to guide the retreatant to a place on the spiritual path that is more fully human and fully alive. The retreat director does not make a judgment or pronounce a verdict, but rather encourages the retreatant to view the situation in a different way and pursue another option, including the encouragement to seek professional help if necessary. In such a circumstance the retreat director is gentle and restrained when making judgments, and open to the possibility that what is understood as an obstacle may in fact be something entirely other than an obstacle—it could even be a profound opportunity for grace.

Admittedly the relationship between a retreat director and the person on retreat is a profoundly different experience than other relationships in life. In other relationships, where the primary relationship may be to teach, admonish, inform, or even evangelize, a different dynamic comes into play. It is important that the distinction is respected and understood by each person.

That being stated, there are, to be honest, specific retreat formats and experiences in which the primary relationship between the retreat director and the retreatant is not what has been described above. For example, a retreat that has been advertised and promoted within a specific religious denomination, with a specific theme and stated goals and objectives, could be an entirely different experience.

There are retreat weekends that have been designed specifically for the purpose of teaching and evangelizing. A retreat director conducting a retreat with this stated purpose may well not be open to conflicting opinions or values, some of which may be in opposition to dogmatic pronouncements and doctrine of the particular denomination that he or she represents. In this case, it would be unrealistic to expect a dynamic such as I described above.

A person who commits to a retreat that teaches the basic principles of Zen Buddhism will be expected to follow the teaching and the directives of the *Roshi*. The role of the Roshi teacher is to guide, form, correct, and admonish. It would be unrealistic to expect that a person could enter into a conversation with a Roshi, suggesting a variation on an essential practice and expect that the Roshi would be encouraging and open to the suggestion. That is not the role of the Roshi and it is most certainly not reflective of the dynamic between teacher and student.

In addition to the skill and the posture of the retreat director other variables are also worth noting. The personality, theology, and the spiritual practice of the retreat director are also very important considerations for a person who seeks to be guided.

There are certain retreat directors that an individual person may prefer and still others that are quite capable and professional but perhaps not as appealing to the retreatant. The dynamics of human relationships, likes and dislikes, assumptions and presumptions, are all components of the retreat experience and of the retreat director. There are simply some types of personalities that an individual person may prefer and there are other personality types that a person may not be particularly attracted to. The dynamic comes into play for both the retreatant and the retreat director.

If, as a retreat director, the encounter with the individual retreatant is limited to the experience of a weekend retreat, personality is not normally that important and does not usually come into play. However, if the experience will be potentially longer than a single encounter, and has the possibility of evolving into an ongoing relationship of prolonged spiritual direction, that is an entirely different story. A mutually agreed upon starting point becomes very important in this instance.

I have discovered in my experience that at the beginning of a spiritual direction relationship a ground rule that is very helpful is for the retreatant and the director to give each other permission to end the relationship *for any reason whatsoever.* In other words, the relationship is constructed on the basic of mutual respect for each other, a respect that permits each person to end the relationship, without the expectation of explaining the whys and the wherefores. The ability to simply end the relationship gives to each person a necessary freedom that enhances and enables the relationship. It is an experience and an expectation that is so "other" that it makes the spiritual direction relationship a special encounter for each person.

In addition to personality considerations, theological considerations are also very important. A person's understanding of God, including all the perceptions, assumptions, judgments, dogmas, and anything else that may be associated with their personal understanding is crucial to the relationship. There must be some point of mutual convergence, some sharing of a common path and experience, if the relationship is to be beneficial to both the retreatant and the retreat director.

Something of the theology of the retreat director will be revealed in any of the formal presentations that he or she may share with the group. It may be within the context of the theme of the retreat, it may be within the context of a liturgical service, or it may be revealed in a sermon or homily. Each of these experiences may be very helpful in coming to at least a beginning appreciation of a theological position.

The corporate sponsor of the retreat center, the congregation, community, or board of directors of the retreat center also contribute to the theological position of the people who may be on the retreat center staff. If you are unsure of their perception, it is useful to ask to see the mission statement of the retreat center. If a mission statement is unavailable, or if you prefer not to be that direct, another place to get some insight into the theology of the retreat center and possibly of the retreat directors, is to visit the bookstore of the center. Take a quick inventory of the titles and the publishers that are displayed and if you feel comfortable with the books, chances are you will also feel comfortable with the retreat directors, who often recommend, or in some instances are responsible for purchasing the books that are available.

A final consideration is the spiritual practice of the retreat director. An effective director shares with you their experience of God and of the spiritual journey and does not simply report to you what they have learned. There is a difference between sharing and reporting. For me this point has been made abundantly clear through the examination of evaluation forms that are routinely provided to retreatants at the end of their experience. Again and again as I read through the evaluation forms, a common theme emerges. People routinely compliment most of the retreat directors and the professionalism with which they approach their subject, but they single out those directors who seem to have something more. The something more that captures their praise and perhaps engages their own spiritual quest in a way that may come as a surprise to them is when they recognize in the retreat director authentic, direct, and personal experience with the spiritual path. There is no substitute for experience.

When all is said and done, a retreat experience can certainly be enhanced through the ministry of a caring and qualified retreat director. It also can be asserted that a director that is less than prepared or who simply does not click with the retreatant can negatively impact the experience. However, that being said, what is truly important and lasting from the experience should ultimately have little or nothing to do with the director. I can easily recall my own retreat experiences, specific moments of insight received and blessings recognized, and at the same time have difficulty identifying the retreat director with the retreat. The retreat director is important, and although it is worth the effort to find a director that will be the most helpful to you, it is not a catastrophe if the choice does not work out as planned or hoped for. After all, as Saint Paul reminds us, "But if it is by grace, it is no longer on the basis of works; otherwise grace would no longer be grace" (Rom 11:6).

CHAPTER **TWELVE**

AFTER YOUR RETREAT, THE LAUNDRY WILL STILL BE WAITING

You know that I like all that I am hearing.
You know that I find the world too busy.
My life is too busy.
Everything geared toward success, and away from you.
You know that I'm resonating with everything that I am hearing.
Please, God…once I am back home:
Don't let me forget.
—Jeanette Angell, *All Ground Is Holy*
(Morehouse Publishing, 1993)

Attach yourself to the blessed Creator,
And in that state of deveikut (connection to God)
Pray for some household need...
Even though there is no immediate need for it.
Do this in order to train yourself
To keep your mind connected to the blessed Creator,
Even when it comes to mundane matters.
This practice will help you
Maintain your deveikut at all times.
—Tzav'at HaRivask, #81,
taken from God In All Moments by Or Rose and Ebn Leader
(Jewish Lights Publishing, 2004)

I enjoy washing dishes. I enjoy washing dishes because there is a beginning, a middle, and an end to the process. I know how to sort and stack the dishes. I know how to scrape the accumulated garbage off of the dinner plates and even how to remove the baked on food that remains in the casserole dish. I know where every dish needs to be placed in the kitchen cupboard after they have been washed and dried. When I have completed the task I can stand back, hang the towel up to dry, and walk away with a sense of satisfaction and a real sense of completion.

I experience the same sense of satisfaction and completion with many of the other simple tasks in life that I routinely engage in; I seldom experience a parallel sense of satisfaction and completion at the end of a retreat.

Although a retreat has a definite beginning, middle, and an end within the context of the time devoted to the retreat, the content of the retreat does not. The subject matter that has been discussed, the specific skills that have been practiced, and the slowly evolving openness to the spiritual process does not end when you drive away at the end of the retreat. A certain experience of retreat may be a new beginning. Yet another experience of retreat may speak best to the middle of the spiritual journey. Still other retreats signal the end of one perspective, while at the same time the retreat introduces the retreatant to yet another new beginning, and the cycle therefore continues.

Regardless of whether the retreatant believes his or her position on the spiritual journey as at the beginning, the middle, or the end, the person who arrives at a retreat center at the start of the retreat experience is not the same as the person who will leave the retreat center when it is completed. For each and every person who participates in the retreat, the experience will change him or her in some way. For some the change will be quite simple, while for others it will be a very dramatic change. For some the experience will be the beginning of what may evolve into an extended relationship with the staff of a particular retreat center. For others the experience of the retreat is part of the "middle" of their spiritual journey, a tool that is used and appreciated. For still others the experience may well be the end, at least at this point in their lives, because their needs may not have been met or they are ready to move on to something else.

There are other thoughts and feelings that a person may find themselves reflecting on at the conclusion of the retreat that have nothing to do with beginnings or endings. The change that is experienced can have other interpretations and offer a multitude of perspectives.

The simplest change experienced may well be the satisfaction of knowing that you have been somehow reconnected to the spiritual sense of who you are as a person. The retreat experience served as a shot in the arm, just the right amount of encouragement needed to continue developing your relationship with God. The time set aside for the retreat helped you to more clearly focus on certain priorities in life and helped you recommit to the spiritual practices with which you are familiar and you find comforting. As you leave the center you have a sense of knowing that you can seek a retreat again, sometime in the future when you need to be energized, but for the most part the daily routine of your own spiritual practice is very fulfilling.

Another common reaction, often reported by those who have engaged in the retreat experience, illustrates a change that may be a little more profound. During the retreat a specific theological point, essential to your religious tradition or spiritual practice, may have been clearly explained or a personal understanding clarified. Or perhaps a specific blockage, something that caused you repeated difficulty or discouragement, was explored and a technique or skill discovered that placed it into proper perspective. If this description feels right to you, then the time spent on retreat provided you with a specific result that enables you to continue with more confidence in your spiritual practice. As you leave the center there is a real sense of accomplishment, perhaps a certain bounce in your step, and you may enjoy a reinforced sense of purpose and direction.

But you may have chosen a retreat in order to accomplish a specific goal, for example to enjoy a period of time in close proximity to the sacred, or even to spend some time with other people who are also spiritual seekers. In this instance an unexpected change may have also occurred when the specific goal soon gave way to an unplanned and surprising result. What you expected from the retreat turned out to be the most insignificant result and in addition to the original goal, you discovered a skill, an insight, or perhaps a spiritual director or mentor that led them in a completely different direction. What you perhaps experienced was a spiritual breakthrough, something that was unplanned for, a moment of grace perhaps, and the retreat may become a defining moment of growth on your path of the spiritual journey.

In addition to each of these common occurrences there are still other experiences that are encountered during a retreat. Other experiences that move a person in a response to the sacred we might understand as dramatic and life changing.

I can remember one retreat weekend of a few years ago when during the planned presentations the retreat director spoke about the importance of dreams. The retreat group listened with some interest to his explanation, and in the period of questioning one of the retreatants asked if he or she could share with the group a particular dream for possible interpretation and some useful insight. The retreat director and the group agreed to the necessary "what is shared in this room stays in this room" condition for self-disclosure and the dream was presented. The group reacted with great reverence as the dream was shared because it soon became obvious to all that the dream was sacred. The person who shared the dream was not unaware of the sacred dimension of the dream but up until the moment of sharing the dream was reluctant to assign significant meaning to it. The reaction of the presenter and the group helped the person become aware of the great gift he had received and, with the additional help of the retreat director in private conversation, to begin to understand an appropriate response. Needless to say the entire experience was dramatic for all and life changing for the person who shared the dream.

On another occasion, I can remember a retreat weekend when I was sharing a conference style, preached retreat with another retreat director. Approximately one hundred people were in attendance for the weekend and from my perspective were entering into the spirit of what we were trying to accomplish. However, one person, sitting in one of the last seats in the back of the room, seemed to be uncomfortable with the process—when others would smile or laugh, he looked like he was not making the connection. From my viewpoint I judged that he was perhaps unhappy and I became concerned that this was something that could not be ignored and would probably be addressed sometime during the weekend.

Midway through the retreat conference on Saturday afternoon, before the designated time for questions and discussions, suddenly his hand went up in the air and he asked to be recognized. We did so, fully expecting that this moment would be the moment when his displeasure was shared with all. Instead of displeasure, however, he shared with the group something completely other than we expected. "I reluctantly came to this retreat because my wife thought it was a good idea for me to be here. I initially resisted everything you were sharing with us but, as I sat here listening, I have slowly become aware of another reality. I recognize that I am like a man who has been overcome with thirst, so thirsty that I did not even know what state I am in, and now I am confronted with a fountain of water, overflowing all around me, and I just can't get enough of it!"

Your retreat may produce a variety of powerful emotions and feelings and your retreat may also produce other reactions that, although perhaps not as dramatic as the dreamer or the person who had their thirst slaked, are nevertheless important. For example, whatever your experience of the retreat, a shared reality for all those who spend time in retreat is that the atmosphere and the conditions that are present in the retreat center are not easily duplicated outside of the center. The lack of silence, solitude, and easy access to many things spiritual can become a significant challenge in the normal day-to-day experience of life. Faced with these obstacles, people may mistakenly conclude that the spiritual practice engaged in during the retreat is only possible within the retreat center and not supported outside of the center.

Although it is true that some components of the retreat cannot be easily sustained outside of the retreat center, the components that can be sustained and nourished are also very much present. The emphasis that a person takes with them at the end of the retreat should not be on what cannot be supported or duplicated but rather an emphasis on what can be accomplished.

Something as simple as determining that upon your arrival home you will find and designate a place in your home as a prayer corner, for example, can be a very valuable step. Such a designation does not have to be dramatic, entailing the moving of furniture or knocking out a wall. A good start might be to put a candle on the table next to a spiritual book of importance to you or next to the sacred scriptures. This simple designation serves as a reminder of your need to pray and also provides an atmosphere for prayer when you take time to light the candle and discover a quiet place to reflect and to meditate.

In addition to a prayer corner, it is also helpful to determine a specific time of day, and a specific length of time to be spent in meditation and prayer. Designating a special time for prayer helps a person develop the habit and the discipline of prayer, not unlike the structure provided at the retreat center with the schedule of the day. As the habit of prayer and meditation is developed, the time that was initially so hard to find becomes an effortless and spiritually enriching sacred refuge.

In addition to the prayer corner and the specific time of day for prayer, it is also important to give yourself "permission" to engage in prayer. At first this may seem a little strange, but if you think about it, you will see the wisdom of this step. Much of the quality and important activity in our lives is chosen. We place ourselves into a position where it is possible to accomplish what we have set out to do. If the necessary time is not scheduled, if we do not make the necessary arrangements, often what happens, despite our best intentions, is that the day just passes by and the opportunity is no longer present. When we give ourselves permission to incorporate prayer and meditation into our daily routine, it has a much better chance of taking root.

In addition to giving ourselves permission, we might also learn to be patient with ourselves as the habit and the discipline slowly develops. The initial fervor and dedication that often follows the spiritual excitement of the retreat can easily begin to slip away. The energy and the enthusiasm that was present on the first day after the retreat may not be as obvious on the tenth day, or the twenty-fifth day, and so on. Regardless of how slowly the discipline and the habit may develop, even to the point where both our candle and our holy book may be covered with dust, we can nevertheless return and profit from the spiritual discipline at any time.

Finally, even with the most spiritual persons, there are the necessary and practical things in life that still need to be attended to. The retreat experience may have been a significant turning point in your life, you may find yourself enthusiastically on the spiritual path, but the dirty clothes still pile up, the dishes still need to be washed and dried, and the normal and regular routines in life still demand your attention. However, what you may discover is that with a new spiritual attitude and a growing awareness and experience of awakening within you, each of these normal and everyday functions can take on new meaning and purpose.

PART THREE

RESOURCES

GETTING READY TO PRAY

A PRACTICAL MODEL FOR ENTERING INTO PRAYER

1. Choose a specific and suitable place to pray, a place where you feel comfortable and where you will experience the fewest interruptions.

2. Take a moment to become relaxed, become aware of the rhythm of your breathing and permit the rhythm to slowly calm you and free you from the anxiety and the concerns of the day.

3. With each breath that you inhale, permit the spirit of God to enter into you; with each breath that you exhale, let go of concerns, worry, and anxiety.

4. Recall the presence of God, in whatever way you understand God, and let that presence be gently with you.

5. Permit all of your thoughts to simply flow past your attention, not unlike a river slowly passing before you.

6. Enter into the silence and let the silence be present to you.

7. When you feel ready, gently become aware of other sounds around you and slowly permit the silence to recede, fully aware that you can return again in prayer.

8. Rest for a moment before you return to the thoughts and concerns of the day.

NOTE: On those occasions when the silence may be difficult to experience or when you are in need of specific direction or inspiration, step six can include the meditative reading of scripture or the writings of a spiritual mentor. Choose to read only a small section, pause and reflect on a single word or thought that may have captured your imagination. When ready, return at least for a moment to the silence before moving on to step seven.

SCRIPTURE PASSAGES
FOR REFLECTION

Scripture passages often present us with an opportunity to pray with another, to join our thoughts with their thoughts. Even though the feelings and the hopes that are expressed are thousands of years old, they nevertheless succeed in adequately describing our special needs and desires. Such prayers are also very useful as a springboard for our own prayer.

Isaiah 43:1–7	You are precious in my eyes.
1 Samuel 3:1–18	Speak Lord, your servant is listening.
Psalm 40	To do your will is my desire.
Psalm 42	My soul thirsts for the living God.
Psalm 51	Have mercy, O God, have mercy.
Psalm 139	Truly you have formed my inmost being.
Wisdom 11:21–27	Lord, you love all that exists.
Luke 1:26–38	My soul proclaims the glory of the Lord.
Ephesians 2:11–18	Through Jesus we possess the way to the Father.
Romans 8: 28–39	Nothing shall separate us from the love of God.

Sometimes when we come to prayer we may discover within ourselves a dominant thought or feeling that seems to be immediately present to us. It is often useful to acknowledge such strong feelings instead of ignoring them or trying to put them to the side for another day. Within the spiritual tradition there is an operating assumption that the presence of a strong preference may well be the voice of

God or the call of the spirit of the Lord. The following readings may resonate with particular moods and provide insight into the mind of God.

Trust	Luke 1:26–38	Let it be done to me as you say.
Weariness	Psalm 62	How long, O Lord?
A Desire to Pray	Luke 11:1–13	Teach us to pray.
Praise God	Psalm 96	Let the heavens be glad.
Thankfulness	Psalm 92	You have made me glad, Lord.
Close to the Lord	John 15:15–17	You are my friend.
Fear	Isaiah 44:1–5	Be not afraid.
Confusion	Psalm 25	Make me know your ways.
Hope	Romans 8:28–39	Who can be against us?
A Call to Serve	Acts 22:3–16	What must I do Lord?
Waiting	Psalm 40	I have waited for the Lord.
Patience	James 5: 7–11	Lord, give me patience.
Memory	Psalm 136	Remember the Lord.
Healing	1 Corinthians 12:4–11	The Spirit heals.
Thirst for God	Psalm 42	My soul thirsts for God.

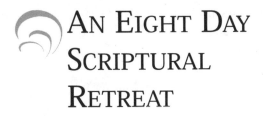

An Eight Day Scriptural Retreat

The following eight-day retreat introduces a retreatant to some of the important themes for reflection and prayer that are commonly meditated on during the time of retreat. The themes build on each other and contain within them a movement to awareness and appreciation of the activity of God at work within a person. The suggested readings from scripture for each of the eight days are intended to help focus attention: it is not necessary or required to complete all of the suggested readings for each of the days. It is helpful, for discussion with the retreat director or at a future time with a spiritual director, to make appropriate notes for each day of retreat. Commonly these notes would include some of the thoughts, feelings, and emotions that may have been experienced by the retreatant during the formal periods of prayer and reflection.

First Day of Retreat: God has created me and called me into life.
Suggested Scripture: Psalm 139:1–8; Jeremiah 18:1–10; Psalm 8.

Second Day of Retreat: I am loved by God.
Suggested Scripture: 1 John 4:7–19; Romans 8:26–34; Psalm 23; Romans 5:1–11.

Third Day of Retreat: God desires to be in relationship with me.
Suggested Scripture: Isaiah 43:1–4 and 49: 13–16; John 14: 16–28.

FOURTH DAY OF RETREAT: All that I have has been given to me by God.
Suggested Scripture: James 1:16–19; 2 Corinthians 4: 5–18;
John 15:1–8.

FIFTH DAY OF RETREAT: God will forgive me my transgressions and sins.
Suggested Scripture: Psalm 103; Luke 18:9–14; Romans 8:28–39

SIXTH DAY OF RETREAT: God calls me to live in freedom.
Suggested Scripture: Psalm 42; Hebrews 11:8–19;
Philippians 3:7–16.

SEVENTH DAY OF RETREAT: I am called by God to build the kingdom of God.
Suggested Scripture: John 3:22–30; 2 Corinthians 12: 1–10;
Luke 1:26–38.

EIGHTH DAY OF RETREAT: I desire to follow Jesus
Suggested Scripture: Matthew 8: 18–27;
1 Corinthians 1:17–31; Matthew 15.

A HOMEMADE RETREAT

A HELPFUL SPIRITUAL
PLAN FOR A RETREAT—

OF A **DAY**, A **WEEK**,
A **MONTH**—

**FOR WHATEVER WORKS
FOR YOU.**

Prophets and religious teachers are like signs on the road, to
guide spiritual travelers who become lost in the desert. But
those who have attained union with God need nothing but their
inner eye and the divine lamp of faith; they need no signs or
even a road to travel along. Such people
then become signs for others.
— **Rumi, Masnavi II:3312–14**

1. Chose a great spiritual teacher as your day by day mentor. If you
cannot think of one, there are ten suggested companions in the
next section that would be excellent.

2. Lay out a simple daily schedule of meditation, reading, and silence
that you can easily follow.

3. Set aside in your schedule a short time for reading from a book by
or about the mentor you have chosen.

4. To focus your day chose a simple prayer—perhaps no longer than
a single line—that you can repeat more than once during the day.

TEN COMPANIONS
FOR THE JOURNEY

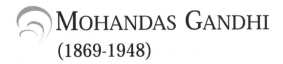

MOHANDAS GANDHI
(1869-1948)

Gandhi is one of the most important voices of the twentieth century. As leader of the Indian independence movement he witnessed to the power of nonviolence, a witness that heavily influenced Dr. Martin Luther King, Jr. and others who were active in the civil rights movement in the United States and throughout the world. A man of deep spirituality, he believed that the search for justice and peace was primarily a search for the fullness of God.

> **MEDITATION:** Let our first act be every morning to make the following resolve for the day: "I shall not fear anyone on earth, I shall fear only God; I shall not bear ill will toward anyone. I shall not submit to injustice from anyone. I shall conquer untruth by truth and in resisting untruth I shall put up with suffering."
> **—May 4, 1919, The Collected Works, vol. 15.**

RECOMMENDED READING:

Brown, Judith M., *Gandhi: Prisoner of Hope*, Yale University Press (New Haven, Ct), 1989.

Dear, John, *Mohandas Gandhi: Essential Writings*, Orbis Books (Maryknoll, NY), 2002.

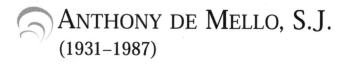

ANTHONY DE MELLO, S.J.
(1931–1987)

A Jesuit priest and spiritual director, Father de Mello succeeded in helping people move beyond the God of words and dogma and experience the personal presence of God in their lives. A storyteller par excellence, he encouraged people to "wake up," and see life in a new and different way. Today, even after his untimely death, he continues to be held in high esteem by many who look to him for direction and guidance on their spiritual path.

Meditation: To love God with one's whole heart means to say a wholehearted yes to life and all that life brings with it. To accept, without reservations, all that God has ordained for one's life. To have the attitude that Jesus had when he said, "Not my will but yours be done."

—The Song of the Bird

Recommended Reading:

de Mello, Anthony, *Sadhana: A Way to God*, Doubleday-Image (New York, NY), 1978.

Dych, William and de Mello, Anthony, *Anthony de Mello: Writings*, Orbis Books (Maryknoll, NY), 1999.

 CHARLES DE FOUCAULD
(1858–1916)

Born into an aristocratic family in France, a life of wealth and privilege was not his intended purpose. Rather, he chose a life of profound and simple witness to the way of "my brother, Jesus." Living among the Muslim poor of Algeria he was murdered, the victim of a random act of violence. After his death, numerous men and women were inspired by his profound writings and life. His spirit and charism lives on today in the lives and the witness of the Little Brothers and the Little Sisters of Jesus.

> **Meditation:** "Fall on your knees, give thanks, adore, bless, weep tears of gratitude, weep with emotion and gratitude, loose yourself in amazed thankfulness…and be careful not to undo what God has done … to separate what God has joined."
> **—Soldier of the Spirit**

Recommended Reading:

Carrouges, Michael, translated by Marie-Christine Hellin, *Soldier of the Spirit: The Life of Charles de Foucauld,* G.P. Putnam and Sons (New York, NY), 1956.

Ellsberg, Robert and de Foucauld, Charles, *Charles de Foucauld: Writings,* Orbis Books (Maryknoll, NY), 1999.

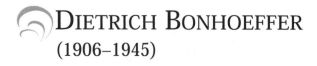

DIETRICH BONHOEFFER
(1906–1945)

A devout Lutheran scholar, theologian, and pastor, his life was completely changed, while at the same time defined, as a result of the rise of Hitler and the Nazis. He refused to be swayed or influenced by a culture that demanded that he forget his Christian commitment, and when faced with a choice, he chose the life of Christ. For this choice, he paid the ultimate price. The cost of his discipleship was a Nazi firing squad.

> **Meditation:** "We hold fast in faith to God's greatest gift, that God has acted for us all and wants to act for us all. This makes us joyful and happy, but it also makes us ready to forgo all such experiences if at times God does not grant them. We are bound together by faith, not by experience."
> **—Life Together**

Recommended Reading:

Bonhoeffer, Dietrich, translated by R.H. Fuller, *The Cost of Discipleship*, Macmillian (New York, NY), 1963.

Coles, Robert and Bonhoeffer, Dietrich, *Dietrich Bonhoeffer: Writings*, Orbis Books (Maryknoll, NY), 1998.

SAINT CATHERINE OF SIENA
(1347–1380)

At a very young age Catherine experienced her first vision of God and, as a result of the vision, dedicated her life to solitary prayer and fasting. At the same time she was also an active woman of faith serving in homes and hospitals as a nurse. Although unable to write, she dictated her teaching and reflections on prayer, obedience, necessary discipline, and other related spiritual topics to friends and members of her family. She had a profound influence on the life of the church in her day and is acclaimed as both as saint and a doctor of the church.

> **Meditation:** "Thanks, thanks be to you ... that you have shown us such great love by fashioning us with these gracious powers in our soul: intelligence to know you; memory to keep you in mind, to hold you within ourselves; will and love to love you more than anything else."

Recommended Reading:

Saint Catherine of Siena, translated by Suzanne Noffke, *The Dialogue*, Paulist Press, (Mahwah, NJ), 1980.

Van der Plancke, Chantal and Knockaert, Andre, *15 Days of Prayer with Saint Catherine of Siena*, Liguori Publications (Liguori, MO), 2000.

SAINT THÉRÈSE OF LISIEUX
(1873–1897)

A young woman, dead at the early age of twenty-four, Thérèse and her "little way," have made her one of the most beloved of saints. A Carmelite nun who led a cloistered life from the age of fifteen, her short life was filled with the music of knowing that she was loved by God—it was also a life of intense moments when she doubted her faith in God, and still other moments when she felt that God had abandoned her. Through it all she prevailed, and at the moment of death pronounced, "My God, I love you."

> **Meditation:** "Your love advised me from as early on as my childhood; it grew with me, and now it is an abyss so deep that I can't measure it's depth. Love attracts love...My love throws itself toward you."

Recommended Reading:

Chalon, Jean, *Thérèse of Lisieux: A Life of Love*, Liguori Publications (Liguori, MO), 1997.

Saint Thérèse of Lisieux, translated by John Clark, *Story of a Soul*, 3rd ed. ICS Publications (Washington, D.C.), 1996.

⟩SAINT JOHN OF THE CROSS
(1542–1591)

J ohn of the Cross was a great mystical theologian, poet, Carmelite monk, reformer, and priest. John believed that mystical union with God, the center of the Christian life, is attained through a life of purest constancy in faith and love. With single-minded devotion, despite numerous times of discouragement, imprisonment, and almost nonstop harassment, he persisted on his chosen spiritual path.

> **Meditation:** "Here are two signs from which we could strongly recognize if God has truly ravished our heart. Is he the object of our ardent desires? Do we experience nothing outside of him? Our heart can only experience peace and rest if it has an object of affection .... That is the condition of a heart that is enflamed with love."

Recommended Reading:

Lyddon, Eileen, *Door Through Darkness: John of the Cross and Mysticism in Everyday Life,* New City Press (New York, NY), 1995.

Tonnelier, Constant, *15 Days of Prayer with Saint John of the Cross*, Liguori Publications (Liguori, MO), 2000.

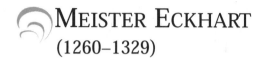MEISTER ECKHART
(1260–1329)

Today acclaimed as a great spiritual master, but in his lifetime he was viewed by many as a heretical teacher of theology and the spiritual path. The root cause of the presumption of heresy was his insistence that God was absolutely transcendent and unknowable, beyond human definitions and dogmatic pronouncements. Eckhart also believed that if we lay aside our lives of sin and cooperate fully with the grace of God, we might nevertheless achieve mystical union with God through contemplation.

Meditation: "All things have a why, but God doesn't have a why, and the person who asks God for anything other than himself, makes God become a 'why.'"

Recommended Reading:

Eckhart, Meister, *The Best of Meister Eckhart*, Ed. Halcyon Backhouse, Crossroad (New York, NY), 1993.

_____, translated by Matthew Fox, *Breakthrough: Meister Eckhart's Creation Spirituality in New Translation*, Doubleday (New York, NY), 1980.

SAINT TERESA OF AVILA
(1515–1582)

T eresa of Avila, a 16th century Carmelite nun and contemporary and friend of Saint John of the Cross, was a woman who could not be easily discouraged. Despite numerous hardships, and despite being a woman in a century that was not easily responsive to the teachings of a woman who "seemed out of her place," she exercised tremendous influence in the teaching of mystical prayer. She authored spiritual classics on prayer and contemplation, reformed her religious community, and served as a spiritual director.

> **Meditation:** "Let nothing disturb you. Nothing dismay you. All things pass. But God never changes. Whoever has God lacks nothing. If you have only God, you have more than enough."

Recommended Reading:

Kirvan, John, *Let Nothing Disturb You: A Journey To the Center of the Soul with Saint Teresa of Avila*, Ave Maria Press (Notre Dame, IN), 1996.

Saint Teresa of Avila, *The Interior Castle*, Doubleday-Image (New York, NY), 1968.

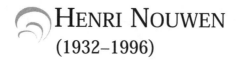Henri Nouwen
(1932–1996)

A prolific writer, teacher, and spiritual director whom many people continue to turn to for guidance in their own spiritual practice and journey. A passionate man, loved by many, he was also personally tormented with loneliness and suffered greatly. Through it all he maintained a generous spirit of heart and soul and a willingness to share with others his own life experience and his deep faith.

> **Meditation:** Wherever I am, at home, in a hotel, in a train, plane or airport, I would not feel irritated, restless, and desirous of being somewhere else or doing something else. I would know that here and now is what counts and is important because it is God himself who wants me at this time in this place.
> **—Genesee Diary**

Recommended Reading:

Nouwen, Henri, *Reaching Out: The Three Movements of the Spiritual Life*, Doubleday (New York, NY), 1966.

_____, *Life of the Beloved: Spiritual Living in a Secular World*, Crossroad (New York, NY), 1996.

TYPICAL RETREAT SCHEDULES

HERE ARE A FEW EXAMPLES OF
BASIC PROGRAMS FOLLOWED AT
RETREAT CENTERS.

Basic Retreat Schedule

7:00 AM	Rising
7:30	Morning prayer (Mass)
8:15	Breakfast
9:15	Retreat conference
10:15	Devotions
11:15	Second conference
12:00 PM	Lunch and rest, exercise
2:30	Third conference
3:30	Devotions
5:00	Evening prayer
5:30	Dinner
7:00	Fourth conference with discussion
8:30	Night prayer

Directed Retreat

7:00 AM	First formal prayer period
8:15	Breakfast in silence
9:15	Walking contemplation
10:15	Second formal prayer period
11:30	Meeting with director
12:30	PM Lunch, followed by rest and exercise
2:30	Third formal prayer period
3:30	Walking contemplation
5:30	Dinner
7:00	Fourth formal prayer period
8:30	Reflection, journaling, prepare for bed

Zen Sesshin Schedule

4:00 AM	Rising
4:30	Zazen
4:55	Kentan *
5:05	Dokusan *
6:30	Breakfast
7:00	Work, rest
9:00	Sutras *
9:30	Zazen
10:30	Extended Kinhin *
11:00	Zazen
12:00 PM	Lunch
12:30	Work, rest
2:00	Zazen
2:30	Teisho *
3:15	Dokusan
4:30	Extended Kinhin
5:00 PM	Shodoka *
5:30	Dinner
6:00	Work, rest
7:00	Zazen
7:30	Dokusan
8:50	Closing, retire for the day

Ten Best Internet Resources

www.expandretreats.com

This Web site offers a directory of retreat and renewal centers for their client members. It includes not only a brief description of the retreat center, but also a direct e-mail link to a designated contact person at the retreat center, and especially welcome, links directly to the retreat centers that offer specific retreats that you may be interested in.

www.findthedivine.com

A wealth of information is offered at this site, and it is constantly updated and improved. Not only can you locate a particular retreat center by region and program, this site provides additional resources for those who are seeking general knowledge about spirituality. Particularly helpful and unique to this site is a directory of spiritual directors—men and women who are willing to join their efforts with yours on the journey of spiritual discovery.

www.tatfoundation.org

This site provides an international directory of places that are conducive to the solitary retreat experience. It provides listings of hermitages, cabins, tents, huts, and even the occasional chalet, each of which welcome spiritual pilgrims of a variety of religious traditions. Centers that require a specific belief system are not listed. The unique feature of this site is the primary focus on the solitary retreat experience.

www.nardacenters.org

This is the official web site of the North American Retreat Directors Association, a Christian association of retreat and renewal centers and leaders in North America. NARDA centers foster ecumenical relationships, peace, justice, the integrity of creation, international solidarity and global collaboration, and understanding of the gospel in a global context. NARDA retreat and renewal centers are usually associated with denominations that have membership in the World Council of Churches. A parallel web site, featuring primarily Catholic retreat and renewal centers, is Retreats International.

www.retreatsintl.org

This is the official Web site of Retreats International, retreat and renewal centers founded within the Roman Catholic tradition. This site provides a listing of three hundred retreat centers, primarily in the United States and Canada. In addition to the retreat and renewal centers, specific programs and spiritual growth opportunities organized by Retreats International also are featured on the site. A parallel Web site, featuring primarily retreat and renewal centers associated with the World Council of Churches, is NARDA.

www.sacredspace.ie

This Web site entitled "Sacred Space," is hosted by the Irish Jesuits. It is a place intended to provide an oasis, a daily retreat experience, in front of your computer, the place where many people find themselves each day. Specific scripture as well as onscreen guidance and explanation are all part of the experience, designed to fit within a time frame of ten minutes a day. The entire site is unique, but perhaps the option of the use of any one of fifteen languages for your prayer further defines the experience.

www.elatchayyim.org

Elat Chayyim, a Jewish spiritual retreat center located in upstate New York, hosts this Web site. The site not only provides information about Elat Chayyim, but also provides essential contact points for understanding the Jewish contemplative and meditative tradition.

www.1stholistic.com

This Web site provides an almost unlimited resource for people who are interested in holistic and integrated spiritual living. Choose from articles on prayer and spirituality, meditation techniques, and collections of prayers and spiritual practices from a variety of religious traditions. A word of warning: don't go this site unless if you have the time to really browse, there is always something that will capture your imagination and interest.

www.retreatsonline.com

Not as well developed as some of the more established retreat information sites, but is constantly improving. The site features retreat centers, formats, and styles not easily accessible at other sites. If you are looking for a place to retreat in Canada, this might be the site that you check first.

www.godserver.com

This is a unique Web site, really a search engine that can quickly link you to almost any topic of spiritual interest. The resources that are linked to this site are as varied as are the interests and the desires of the human heart. Probably not the place to start if you are more interested in traditional expressions of belief, but if you are searching, it might well be one of the first Web sites that you consider exploring.

Ten Good Books

Brussat, Frederic and Mary Ann, *Spiritual Literacy: Reading the Sacred in Everyday Life*, Touchstone (New York, NY), 1996.

Buxbaum, Yitzhak, *Jewish Spiritual Practices*, Jason Aronson, Inc. (Northvale,NJ), 1994.

de Mello, Anthony, *Awareness*, Doubleday (New York, NY), 1990.

Foster, Nelson and Shoemaker, Jack, *The Roaring Stream: A New Zen Reader*, The Ecco Press (Hopewell, NJ), 1996.

Harvey, Andrew, *A Walk with Four Spiritual Guides*, Skylight Paths Publishing (Woodstock, VT), 2003.

King, Ursula, *Christian Mystics: Their Lives and Legacies Throughout the Ages*, Hidden Spring (Mahwah, NJ), 2001.

Kornfield, Jack, *After the Ecstasy, the Laundry: How the Heart Grows Wise on the Spiritual Path*, Bantam Books (New York, NY), 2000.

Rolheiser, Ronald, *The Holy Longing*, Doubleday (New York, NY), 1999.

Thich Nhat Hanh, *Living Buddha, Living Christ*, Riverhead Books (New York, NY), 1995.

Tolle, Eckhart, *Stillness Speaks*, New World Library (Novato, CA), 2003.

Walsh, Roger, *Essential Spirituality: The 7 Central Practices to Awaken Heart and Mind*, John Wiley & Sons, Inc. (New York, NY), 1999.

Veltri, John, S.J., *Orientations, Volume One: A Collection of Helps for Prayer*, Loyola House (Guelph, Ontario, Canada), 1979. This books is the source for quoted prayers by Thomas Merton, Henry Viscardi, Anselm of Canterbury, and Charles de Foucauld

Prayers

The Road Ahead

My Lord and my God, I have no idea where I am going and I do not see the road ahead of me. I cannot know for certain where it will end. I do not know myself, and the fact that I think that I am following your will does not mean that I am actually doing so. But I believe that the desire to please you is enough, and I hope that is what I am doing. I hope that I will never choose anything that is not your will and that you will lead me on the right path, even though I may not even know that you are leading me. I will trust you always, even though I may seem lost and in the shadow of death. I will not fear, for you are always with me, and will never abandon me.

— Adapted from a prayer of Thomas Merton

Richly Blessed

I asked God for strength, that I might achieve.
I was made weak, that I might learn humbly to obey.
I asked for health, that I might do great things,
I was given infirmity that I might do better things.
I asked for riches, that I might be happy.
I was given poverty that I might be wise.
I asked for power, that I might have the praise of men.
I was given weakness, that I might feel the need for God.
I asked for all things, that I might enjoy life,
I was given life that I might enjoy all things.
I got nothing that I asked for, but everything that I hoped for.
Almost despite myself, my unspoken prayers were answered.
I am, among all men, richly blessed.

— Henry Viscardi

INTO YOUR HANDS

Father, I abandon myself into your hands; do with me what you will.
Whatever you may do, I thank you: I am ready for all, I accept all.
Let only your will be done in me, and in all your creatures.
I wish no more than this, Lord.
Into your hands I commend my soul:
I offer it all to you with all the love of my heart,
For I love you Lord, and so need to give myself, to surrender myself
into your hands without reserve, and with boundless confidence, for
you are my Father.

— Charles de Foucauld

LET ME FIND YOU

Lord my God, teach my heart where and how to seek you and where
and how to find you.
O Lord, you are my God and you are my Lord and I have never seen
you.
You have made me and remade me, and you have bestowed on me all
the good things I possess, and still I do not know you!
I have not yet done that for which I was made.
Teach me to seek you, for I cannot seek you unless you show yourself
to me.
Let me seek you in my desire, let me desire you in my seeking.
Let me find you by loving you, let me love you when I find you.

— Saint Anselm of Canterbury

SURPRISE ME

Lord, catch me off guard today.
Surprise me with some moment of beauty or pain
So that at least for the moment
I may be startled into seeing that you are here in all your splendor,
Always and everywhere,
Barely hidden,
Beneath,
Beyond,
Within this life I breathe.

— Frederick Buechner

LATE HAVE I LOVED YOU

Late have I loved you, O Beauty, ever ancient, ever new.
Late have I loved you.
For behold you were within me, and I outside.
And I sought you outside
And in my unloveliness fell upon those lovely things that you had made.
You were with me, and I was not with you.
I was kept from you by those,
Yet had they not been in you,
They would not have been at all.
You did call and cry to me to break open my deafness
And you did send forth your beams to shine upon me
And chase away my blindness.
You breathed fragrance upon me,
And I drew my breath and do now pant for you.
I tasted you and now hunger and thirst for you.
You touched me, and I burn for you.

— Saint Augustine

IN BEAUTY

O you who dwell in the house made of the dawn,
In the house made of the evening twilight . . .
Where the dark mist curtains the doorway,
The path to which is on the rainbow . . .
I have made your sacrifice.
I have prepared a smoke for you.
My feet restore for me.
My limbs restore for me.
My body restore for me.
My mind restore for me.
My voice restore for me.
Today, take away your spell from me.
Away from me you have taken it.
Far off from me you have taken it.
Happily I recover.
Happily my interior becomes cool.

Happily my eyes regain their power.
Happily my head becomes cool.
Happily my limbs regain their power.
Happily I hear again.
Happily for me the spell is taken off.
Happily I walk.
Impervious to pain, I walk.
Feeling light within, I walk . . .
In beauty I walk.
With beauty before me, I walk.
With beauty behind me, I walk.
With beauty below me, I walk.
With beauty all around me, I walk.
It is finished in beauty.
It is finished in beauty.
It is finished in beauty.

— A Navajo Indian Prayer

THE VERSE OF THE THRONE

Allah, there is no God but He, the Living, the Eternal.
Neither slumber nor sleep seizes Him.
To Him belongs what is in the heavens and in the earth.
Who can intercede with Him, except by His permission?
He knows what lies before them and after them
and they know nothing of his knowledge, save such as He wills.
His throne encompasses the heavens and the earth
and He never wearies of preserving them.
He is Sublime, the Exalted.

— Koran 2:255

PRAYER FOR ABUNDANCE

May the kingdom of justice prevail!
May the believers be united in love!
May the hearts of the believers be humble, high their wisdom,
And may they be guided in their wisdom by the Lord.
Glory be to God!
Entrust unto the Lord what thou wishest to be accomplished.
The Lord will bring all matters to fulfillment.
Know this as truth evidenced by Himself.

— Sikh Prayer

PRAISE GOD

All that is in the heavens and the earth glorify God;
And He is the Mighty, the wise.
He is the Sovereignty of the heavens and the earth;
He is able to do all things.
He is the First and the Last,
And the Outward and the Inward;
He is the knower of all things.

— Koran 57:1–3

GIVE US

O gracious and holy Father,
Give us wisdom to perceive you,
intelligence to understand you,
diligence to seek you,
patience to wait for you,
eyes to see you,
a heart to meditate on you,
and a life to proclaim you,
through the power of the spirit of Jesus Christ our Lord.

— Saint Benedict

THE UNITY OF LIFE

Those who know do not speak;
Those who speak do not know.
Stop up the openings,
Close down the doors,
Rub off the sharp edges.
Unravel all confusion.
Harmonize the light,
Give up the contention:
This is called finding the unity of life.
When love and hatred cannot affect you,
Profit and loss cannot touch you,
Praise and blame cannot ruffle you,
You are honored by all the world.

— **Lao Tzu**

I LOVE

God, I love Your creativity—
The way You can fill an ordinary day with momentous experiences;
Your ability to turn a bad situation into an occasion for growth;
Your mercy which transforms episodes of sin into encounters with salvation.
I love Your affinity for beauty.
I love Your sense of humor.
I love Your steadfast presence.
I love Your vulnerability.
I love Your comfort.
I love Your commitment to community.
I love Your favor for underdogs.
I love Your passion for ministry, for peace, and for revelation.
I love what You do and who You are.
I love You for being You, God!

— **C. Weldon Gaddy**

DIVINE BLESSING

Almighty Lord, if we offer you a devoted mind and heart, you will offer to us every blessing on earth and in heaven.

You grant our deepest wishes. You give food to the body and peace to the soul. You look upon us with the love of a mother for her children.

You created this beautiful earth all around us. And in every plant and animal, every tree and bird, your spirit dwells.

You have revealed yourself to me, infusing my soul with the knowledge that you are the source of all blessing.

And so I sing your praises day and night. I who am feeble, glorify you who are powerful. I who am nothing, devote myself to you who are everything

— Atharva Veda

THE TRUTH OF GOD

Supreme God, your light is brighter than the sun, your purity whiter than mountain snow, you are present wherever I go.

All people of wisdom praise you. So I too put faith in all your words, knowing that everything you teach is true. Neither the angels in heaven nor the demons in hell can know the perfection of your wisdom, for it is beyond all understanding.

Only your Spirit knows you; only you can know your true self. You are the source of all being, the power of all power, the ruler of all creatures. So you alone understand what you are.

In your mercy reveal to me all that I need to know, in order to find peace and joy. Tell me the truths that are necessary for the world in which I live.

Show me how I can meditate upon you, learning from you the wisdom that I need. I am never tired of hearing you, because your words bring life.

— From the Bhagavad Gita

I RECEIVE YOUR LOVE

Beloved God,

Show me the truth about this.

I now surrender all fears, doubts, and judgments, and invite the light of perfect consciousness to illuminate my path.

Pure love is present here and now, as God lives in every person I meet.

I send love and appreciation to all my associates, knowing with perfect confidence that he or she is guided by the same Great Spirit that guides me.

I am not separate from my brothers and sisters, but one with them.

I trust that my highest good is unfolding before me, and I accept the very best that love and life have to offer.

I am worthy of living in the kingdom of Heaven, even as I walk the earth. I claim it now.

Thank you, God, for loving me infinitely, and opening all doors for the highest good of all concerned. I receive Your love, and magnify it. And so it is.

— Alan Cohen

GLOSSARY

ABBA — An Aramaic word for father, routinely used by children. Also used by Jesus at the moment of a great crisis in his life (Mark 14:30). Two other recorded uses are in the context of prayer, Romans 8:15 and Galatians 4:6.

ABRAHAM — His story is told in the book of Genesis, chapters twelve to twenty-five. Abraham ("father of a multitude" or "exalted father") was born almost two thousand years before Christ, in modern day Iraq. He is known as the Father of the Jewish people and is also considered a great prophet in Islam and Christianity.

BHAGAVAD GITA — The best loved of all of the Hindu scriptures often referenced simply as the Gita, "Song." In English it may best be identified as "The Song of the Beloved or Blessed One." According to Hindu tradition the author of the Gita was the sage Vyasa, (the compiler). It has attained the status of divine revelation within this religious tradition and has been translated into all of the modern languages.

BIBLE — A collection of songs, parables, poetry, teaching stories, and other forms of writing, gathered together into a collection of books, officially recognized and accepted by Christians as the inspired word of God. The Hebrew scriptures (generally referred to as the Old Testament by Christians) is comprised of forty-six books, detailing the relationship between God and Israel before Jesus, while the Christian scriptures (referred to as the New Testament by Christians) has twenty-seven books that are concerned with Jesus and the early church.

CATHOLIC — From the Greek, meaning "universal," it is usually understood as the official title or designation given to the body of Christian communities in union with the pope, the bishop of Rome (thus, Roman Catholics). Saint Ignatius of Antioch first used it in the year 107 as a description of the church.

CONVERSION — The traditional understanding of conversion is to change, or more specifically, to repent of sin. In this discussion we have suggested that perhaps it is better understood as an attitude and a perception towards life. A way of seeing and understanding life that then permeates and animates the choices and the decisions that are daily made. Conversion is a process and a choice, the filter or the lens that is used to perceive and then interpret the world in which we live, from the less to the more, scarcity to abundance.

CONTEMPLATION — "Soul food," the essential nutrient that fuels the spirit of the human person, which then enables the intimate response to the Other, to God. Contemplation is experienced in silence. Saint John of the Cross defines contemplation as the "loving knowledge of God," while Saint Gregory the Great defines it as "resting in God."

DISCERNMENT — In the Christian tradition it is understood as a gift of grace, a specific charism or gift of the Holy Spirit, which permits a person to recognize and identify the specific intention or purpose of God's will, as it is manifested. It is the art of choosing one specific direction from a variety of different ways, all of which are in themselves good and useful.

DOKUSAN — A private interview with teacher or Zen master, typically while participating in a Zen sesshin (retreat).

ENNEAGRAM — From the Greek ennea which means nine and grammos which designates figure: literally, "nine-pointed figure." The Enneagram maps out nine distinct personality types, which are believed to be manifested in the human person and in their individual relationships. Having roots in both psychology and in accumulated ancient spiritual wisdom from a variety of religious traditions— Christian, Buddhist, Sufi, and the Jewish Kabbalah—many people consider it a useful spiritual tool.

GOSPEL — From the Old English word god-spel, traditionally translated as "good news." There are four canonically accepted gospels in the Christian tradition that tell the story of the life, teaching, suffering, death, and resurrection of Jesus Christ. It is customary to describe the Gospels of Matthew, Mark, and Luke as "synoptic Gospels" because they give a "synopsis" or similar view of the life and teaching of Jesus; the Gospel of John reflects a different tradition. In addition to the canonical gospels there are other gospels that were not accepted into the Christian Bible, including, for example, the gospel of Thomas, the gospel of Peter, and the gospel of Mary Magdalene.

HITBODEDUT — A Jewish spiritual practice, the word means "aloneness with God." It is intended to be a daily practice of prayer and devotion.

KABBALAH — Also spelled Cabala. It refers to the mystical interpretation of the Jewish scriptures. The two principal written sources for Kabbalah are a third-century work, the Sefer Yezira, which purports to present a series of monologues given by the patriarch Abraham, and the Zohar, a mystical commentary on the Torah written by Moses de León in the thirteenth century. Kabbalah appears to have started in eleventh century France, and then spread to Spain and elsewhere. It influenced the development of Hasidism in the eighteenth century, and continues to play a role in contemporary Judaism.

KENTAN — A standing bow in the Zen tradition. Hands are clasped in front of the person and when the teacher passes by the bow is made from the waist.

KINHIN — A defined period of walking meditation during a Zen retreat; in contrast to the extended periods of time that are spent sitting in meditation. The time period can be just a few moments or extended for a longer period of time.

KORAN — The holy book accepted by Muslims as the revealed word of Allah to his prophet Muhammad. It provides the divine motivation and interpretation for most religious, social, cultural, and commercial activity in an Islamic society.

LABYRINTH — A designed linear or circular pattern or path, sometimes called the holy walk, which is a sacred symbol that can be traced back at least three thousand years. In the Christian tradition the labyrinth was walked as a symbolic journey to the holy city of Jerusalem, the city sacred to the Jewish people, the Christian people, and the Islamic people. Labyrinths are common in many retreat centers, used as a meditation tool, to help a person focus and encounter the presence of the sacred in their lives.

LITURGY OF THE HOURS — Also called the divine office, this Catholic tradition consists of: morning prayer (Lauds); prayer during the day—before noon (Terce); prayer during the day—midday (Sext); prayer during the day—afternoon (None); evening prayer (Vespers): office of readings (Matins); and night prayer (Compline). Monastic orders pray in community the Liturgy of the Hours each day.

RETREAT — A vacation for the soul. A personal choice and decision to break away from the normal routines of life and to deliberately seek silence, which leads to contemplation, and ultimately to conversion, a new way of seeing and interpreting life from a spiritual perspective.

SAMU — During a Zen sesshin participants are routinely assigned a variety of tasks, identified as "work practice." Meditation continues during the period of work but the task, such as washing dishes, sweeping the meditation room, planting flowers or weeding the garden, is also completed.

SESSHIN, — A retreat in the Zen tradition, the word means "to touch the mind."

SPIRITUAL DIRECTOR — A spiritual companion, mentor, or soul friend experienced and trained in various spiritual traditions, and capable of directing and encouraging another person on their spiritual journey. A good spiritual director encourages and enables the spiritual journey as opposed to dictating or insisting one path over another. The spiritual director stands in awe and respect of the presence and manifestation of God within the person who seeks their help.

Spiritual Exercises — In the general sense, understood as the specific activities that are a part of the retreat experience, i.e. prayer, periods of discussion, preaching, some kind of liturgical ritual, etc. In particular the Spiritual Exercises are understood in reference to the method of spiritual direction and activity established by Saint Ignatius of Loyola in his book of that name, and practiced since then by those who follow the Ignatian method.

Shodoka — The Song of Enlightenment (Cheng-Tao-Ko), a text of seminal importance to Ch'an, Zen, and Taoism. Shodoka is memorized in its entirety by many students in China, Korea and Japan, and it is recited at special occasions.

Sutras — Rules and chants, collected wisdom that are memorized and chanted by Zen students, for example "I venerate the Sacred One, the Great Sage, the Truly Enlightened One."

Teisho — When the teacher or Zen master speaks at a retreat (sesshin), as in a conference or a presentation.

Torah — In Hebrew, though frequently thought of as "law," is better translated as "teaching." This term is commonly used to refer to the Mosaic law as contained in the Pentateuch or first five books of the Bible, namely, Genesis, Exodus, Leviticus, Numbers, and Deuteronomy.

Zazen — In the Zen Buddhist tradition, the term used to denote meditative practice or seated focused awareness.

Zendo — The name that designates the meditation room used in the Zen Buddhist tradition.

Zen Sesshin — A traditional three- to eight-day silent retreat in the Zen Buddhist tradition.

THOMAS SANTA, a Redemptorist priest, is Director of the Redemptorist Renewal Center at Picture Rock, near Tucson, Arizona. There he helped found many innovative retreats including the annual Catholic Writers Retreat and Workshop. For seven years he served as Publisher of Liguori Publications and is the author of seven books, including *Understanding Scrupulosity, Dear Padre: Questions Catholics Ask,* and *Marian Shrines of North America*

Moment By Moment
A Retreat in Everyday Life
Carol Ann Smith, SHCJ
& Eugene F. Merz, SJ
Drawing on the classic retreat model, The Spiritual Exercises of St. Ignatius, Moment by Moment offers a new and inviting way to find God in our often busy and complex lives. Its simple format can be used by an individual or by groups.
ISBN: 0-87793-945-4 / 96 pages / $11.95

Sacred Space
The Prayer Book 2005
Jesuit Communication Centre, Ireland
Sacred Space is a prayer guide inspired by the hugely successful interactive website, www.sacredspace.ie. Both offer a way to reflect and pray each day of the year. Now people everywhere can pray and reflect with **Sacred Space** anytime, anyplace, in just ten minutes a day. Because the prayer book is annual you will be able to continue your prayer journey year after year.
ISBN: 1-59471-030-9 / 384 pages / $12.95

Living In God's Embrace
The Practice of Spiritual Intimacy
Michael Fonseca
Fonseca knows well the difficulties that can arise on the spiritual journey, but he also knows the graces that can come to the ardent seeker. Each chapter is made up of a brief introductory section and ten prayer exercises, guides readers through the ups and downs of the spiritual journey and provides encouragement to stay on the path toward God.
ISBN: 0-87793-939-X / 240 pages / $12.95

Loving In The Master's Footsteps
God's Dream for Us
Michael Fonseca
Guides us to a commitment to Jesus that results in a lifestyle patterned on the Master's teaching and the power of his Spirit. Prayer exercises in each chapter open our hearts fully to the transformation Christ offers us and comfort us with assurances of God's continual desire to be united fully with his people.
ISBN: 0-87793-994-2 / 192 pages / $12.95

KEYCODE: F0T01050000